Brunelleschi

Peter J. Gärtner

Filippo
Brunelleschi

1377–1446

KÖNEMANN

1 (frontispiece)
Santo Spirito, view of the nave (cf. ill. 40)
Piazza Santo Spirito, Florence

© 1998 Könemann Verlagsgesellschaft mbH
Bonner Str. 126, D–50968 Köln

Art Director: Peter Feierabend
Project Manager and Editor: Sally Bald
Assistant: Susanne Hergarden
German Editor: Ute E. Hammer
Assistant: Jeannette Fentroß
Translation from the German: Christian von Arnim
Contributing Editor: Susan M. James
Production Director: Detlev Schaper
Layout: Bärbel Meßmann
Typesetting: Greiner & Reichel, Cologne
Reproductions: Omniascanners, Milan
Printing and Binding: Neue Stalling, Oldenburg
Printed in Germany

ISBN 3-8290-0241-6

10 9 8 7 6 5 4 3 2 1

Contents

BRUNELLESCHI AND EARLY RENAISSANCE FLORENCE

Filippo Brunelleschi's appearance as an architect falls in the period when the initial flowering of Florence was moving into its second heyday. Its first flowering, which we can date to about 1300, includes the construction of Santa Croce by Arnolfo di Cambio (starting in 1295) and the building of Santa Maria Novella, begun by Fra Sisto in 1278. From about 1296 onwards, di Cambio was also in charge of work on the building which was to become the city's largest construction project for 150 years, the cathedral of Santa Maria del Fiore. The sculptors Andrea Pisano and Giotto, properly Giotto di Bondone (1266–1337), who did not work only as a painter, were active in Florence at the time.

From the time that the gold florin was introduced in 1252, the development of Florence into one of the most powerful of Italy's city republics was based on the wealth created by the wool and cloth trade and manufactured articles. Banking was soon included as a further source of prosperity. Nothing quite indicates the importance of Florence so clearly as the fact that the gold coin used as the unit of currency in medieval world trade was simply called the florin.

The Medici were particularly prominent among the Florentine banking families. It is therefore only logical that the second and third flowering of the city should coincide with the lives of two members of that family. From about 1434 onwards, Cosimo de' Medici (1389–1464), the son of Giovanni di Bicci (1360–1429), became the leading personality in the city republic. Under his patronage Florence experienced its second flowering, the start of the early Renaissance: first in sculpture, then in architecture, and finally in painting. Today we can only marvel at the number of famous artists, apart from Brunelleschi, who made their mark on the art of the time. In painting, Masaccio, who lived from 1401 to 1428, deserves to be mentioned in first place; in sculpture, the important names are Lorenzo Ghiberti (1378–1455) and Donatello (1382/86–1466). The highest position among architects undoubtedly belongs to Brunelleschi himself. The mention of these four names only represents the tip of the iceberg. It guides us to another source, however, which provides us with information about the life and work of Brunelleschi as well. This is Giorgio Vasari's "Le vite de più eccellenti Architettori, Pittori e Scultori", which translates as "The Lives of the Most Excellent Painters, Sculptors and Architects", the first edition of which appeared in 1550. Vasari (1511–1574) divides his Lives, which make him into the father of art historiography, into three stages (childhood, youth and maturity) in order to use this framework to show the progression towards the high Renaissance. According to this model, Giotto belongs to the first phase of development, childhood, Brunelleschi and his fellow artists to the second, youth. The third phase, maturity, is dominated by the three great artists of their time: Raphael (1483–1520), Leonardo (1452–1519) and Michelangelo (1475–1564). Vasari's biographies are not unique for this period, and with good reason, even if they are indisputably the best. The rational curiosity which is the hallmark of the Renaissance was directed not only at the legacy of the ancients (rediscovery of the classical period), the world (discovery of America) and physical nature in general (anatomy studies), but also at the individual and his work which is honored in biographical studies. The many biographies and autobiographies which arose are thus – to put it in exaggerated form – the lives of the saints of the modern era. Thus Filippo Brunelleschi also had his enthusiastic biographers: about 1485 Antonio di Tuccio Manetti (1423–1497), who as a young man was still able to meet the old architect, wrote down the story of his life and a catalogue of his work. This is still an important source today. It must be added, however, that Manetti is at his most reliable when he describes actual events, such as building procedures. "Where he becomes the real 'historian' by trying to create causal links between individual events" (Heydenreich), his statements must be viewed more critically. Here his imagination and inventiveness take over.

Filippo Brunelleschi, also known as Filippo di Ser Brunellesco or Pippo di Ser Brunellesco Lippi, was born in Florence in 1377. The less well-known names give a first indication of the family from which he came. His father was a notary, someone who was called *Ser* at that time. Brunellesco Lippi came from a well-off family, as did his wife, Giuliana Spini. The spacious palace of the Spini still stands today opposite Santa Trinità. The

3 Diagram of the city of Florence

The diagram gives an impression of the way Brunelleschi's buildings determine the townscape of Florence. Authentic and preserved works such as the Old Sacristy next to San Lorenzo (No. 8), Santo Spirito (No. 11), the Ospedale degli Innocenti (No. 7) and of course the cathedral (dome, lantern and exedra) (No. 6), buildings and conversions which no longer exist such as Casa Barbadori in Borgo San Jacopo (No. 5), works ascribed to Brunelleschi such as the Barbadori Chapel in Santa Felicità (No. 4) and those which modern research no longer ascribes to him, such as the Palazzo Quaratesi in Via del Proconsolo (No. 15), have been drawn in.

4 View from the Loggia da Sangallo and d'Agnolo to the *Piazza SS. Annunziata* with the portico of the *Ospedale degli Innocenti,* Florence

In the 15th and 16th centuries the open, arched hall, showpiece of the clearly structured façade, which Brunelleschi created for the Ospedale degli Innocenti (Foundling Hospital), initiated one of the most balanced square developments of the Renaissance. Building started in 1419; Brunelleschi was in charge of building until 1427. The two fountains by Pietro Tacca were not built until 1643.

· D · S ·
M · PHILIPPVS · ARCHITECTVS

education which his parents provided for him – he learned to read, write and do arithmetic, as well as Latin – would have enabled him to follow in his father's profession. But he decided differently. In 1398, the twenty-three-year-old applied to the Arte della Seta (Silk Merchants Guild) for acceptance as a goldsmith. His father may have agreed to this training because goldsmiths belonged to the respected and distinguished Silk Guild. In 1404 Brunelleschi was registered as a master goldsmith. Thereafter he seems to have concerned himself mainly with architecture. It is important in this context that as early as 1404 to 1406 he was member of a specialist commission for Florence Cathedral, whose task it was to assess the buttresses for the choir. Filippo Brunelleschi's interest in the building, which was to occupy him as no other in his life, thus began at a very early stage. As early as 1412 he is given the title *capomaestro*, which allows us to conclude that he had been working as an architect for some time.

Nevertheless, we must not forget that Brunelleschi embodied a new type of architect. He was not a mason and never belonged to the masons' guild. An anecdote may show the true significance of this fact. Not belonging to the guild, he was, strictly speaking, not entitled to build. As a consequence, he was arrested in 1434, shortly before the building work on the dome was completed. That he was quickly released again does not change the fact that his arrest was unavoidable because he had been in breach of the regulations. If we also take into account that he is credited with the discovery of centralized perspective, that the vault of the dome of Florence Cathedral is an engineering problem rather than an architectural one, and that Brunelleschi also made his mark as an inventor – the *badalone*, the monster, a project for a transport ship, is ascribed to him – it becomes clear that we encounter in him an *uomo universalis*, a Renaissance man. In the Renaissance view of the artist, it was almost expected that he should be trained to be more than just a painter, sculptor or architect. A painter could work as a sculptor as well as an architect. Thus many artists reveal such diverse talents. We might mention Ghiberti, Brunelleschi and Alberti, or Raphael and Michelangelo. As an *uomo universalis*, Filippo Brunelleschi was subsequently appointed to be the architect and master builder of Florence Cathedral. His selection was not an unusual choice for this city. A hundred years previously, another non-architect – the painter Giotto – had also held this position.

If we look at Brunelleschi's life and work, it becomes clear that after almost 20 years in which he built his reputation as an artist primarily through sculptural work, he suddenly moved into the first rank of architects. About 1420 he is able to start carrying out a notable number of his building designs: the dome of Santa Maria del Fiore, the most impressive and important commission which his home city was able to

award; the *Ospedale degli Innocenti* (Foundling Hospital), a secular building; the *Old Sacristy*, the family chapel of the Medici, and *San Lorenzo*, one of the great sacred buildings of the time. There has been much speculation about what Brunelleschi did in the first two decades of the 15th century and the significance of that period for his building work. We will never be completely certain whether it represents anything more than a long phase of study and intellectual preparation, necessary to make his later work possible. The material evidence is missing – but it is this which makes Brunelleschi's biography so intriguing.

There can be no doubt that the early Renaissance begins with his buildings. Their number is not overwhelming. Most of them can still be seen today in Florence, the city in which the architect worked almost exclusively. This book shows the most important of them, with the exception of the palaces, the *palazzi*. There is one special factor common to the construction of all Brunelleschi's buildings. He only completed a few of them himself and work on them often extended over years and decades. His successors had their own ideas and could not or did not want to follow his specifications. In addition, some of the buildings, such as the Palazzo Pitti, which were ascribed to Brunelleschi in the past, are no longer considered to have been built by him. Nevertheless, Filippo Brunelleschi's buildings have shaped the townscape of Florence (ill. 3). This applies above all, of course, to the dome of the cathedral, Santa Maria del Fiore, which rises above the city's roofs (ill. 2), but also, for example, to the *Ospedale degli Innocenti* at the Piazza SS. Annunziata (ill. 4).

When Brunelleschi died on 14 May 1446 at the age of 69, his contemporaries paid tribute to him and his life's work. The Wool Guild, under whose leadership the lodge of the cathedral masons had been placed, decided not only to bury him in the cathedral, but to honor him further with a memorial bust (ill. 5). This was an innovation, a distinction which no other person had previously enjoyed. Brunelleschi's adopted son, Andrea di Lazzaro Cavalcanti, known as Buggiano, was commissioned to make the bust which was to be placed near the tomb. But even that was not enough. Brunelleschi's drawings of the cathedral dome, which had been preserved, were to be displayed next to the bust together with an inscription honoring his achievements. No less a person than the chancellor of the Florentine republic, Carlo Marsuppini, wrote the inscription and he describes Filippo Brunelleschi as a *divino ingenio*, a "divine creative spirit".

The third flowering of Florence under Lorenzo de' Medici (1449–1492), who placed his mark on the history of the city from 1464 to 1492, and who was significantly called "Il Magnifico", the Magnificent, came after Brunelleschi's lifetime. But the respect which was accorded to him illustrates the significance which artists in the Renaissance were able to achieve.

5 Andrea di Lazzaro Cavalcanti, known as Buggiano
Likeness and inscription on Brunelleschi's tomb, 1446
Santa Maria del Fiore (Cathedral), Florence

According to Vasari, Carlo Marsuppini described the architect as *divino ingenio*, as "divine spirit" in the inscription "which the community had put up to praise him in death having brought honor to his fatherland in life". Long before the *divina artista*, the "divine artist" of the high Renaissance appears, he thus gives an example of the respect which an artist was able to command.

6 Florentine School
Five Famous Men (The Fathers of Perspective),
ca. 1500–1565
Tempera on wood, 42 x 210 cm
Musée du Louvre, Paris

For a long time this painting, which was extensively
overpainted several times, was thought to be the work of
Paolo Uccello. Today this view is increasingly being called
into question and it is therefore no longer dated to the
fifteenth century. Despite the inscription, the figures
shown are not those listed but probably, from left to right,
Antonio Manetti (?), Donatello (?), Paolo Uccello (?),
Masaccio (?) and Filippo Brunelleschi (?). The *Five
Famous Men (The Fathers of Perspective)* were thus a
mathematician, a sculptor, two painters and an architect.
The painting might be modelled on the Masaccio fresco
in the Brancacci Chapel.

7 Masaccio and Filippo Lippi
Raising of the Son of Theophilus and St Peter Enthroned,
1428–1482
Fresco, 232 x 597 cm
Santa Maria del Carmine, Brancacci Chapel, Florence

This detail shows a group of four men thought to be
(from left to right) Masolino, Masaccio, Alberti and
Brunelleschi. They are attendind the enthronement of the
apostle Peter on the episcopal throne. The right-hand side
of the fresco, shown here, which also portays the raising
of the son of Theophilus, is considered Masaccio's own
work and completes the work begun by Filippo Lippi
60 years earlier.

As an architect and artist, Brunelleschi opened up new
ground for Italian art with his work. Onla a few artistic
works have been preserved which show him to be a
forerunner of the Renaissance and place him in the circle of
those famous artists who all performed pioneering work in
their field. These architects, sculptors and painters solved
traditional tasks in unconventional ways and thus provoked
a transformation which was to affect not only Italian art,
but to change European art history as a whole in a fundamental way. Since new developments on this scale in all
areas of fine art occur only rarely, they were studied with
enthusiasm: enormous artistic productivity got underway in
the second half of the fifteenth century. Thus, according to
the chronicler Benedetto Dei, thirty palaces were built in
Florence in the years between 1450 and 1478 and the
number of stonemasons' workshops rose to fifty-four. The
new style soon spread over the whole of Italy, where local
styles gradually began to develop.

An answer to the question as to which artists, apart from
Brunelleschi, were ascribed a decisive role in ushering in
the early Renaissance can be found in literature and
contemporary works of art.

The Florentine humanist, art theorist and architect, Leon
Battista Alberti (1404–1472), dealt with this new artistic
consciousness and style in the second edition of his treatise
on painting "Della pittura libri tre" published in 1436. It
contains a dedication to Brunelleschi at the beginning in
which he also mentions four other names in addition to
Brunelleschi:

"For when I returned to my native city, the most beautiful
of all, after the long exile in which we, the Alberti, have
grown old, I understood for the first time that you Filippo
(Brunelleschi), you my best friend Donato (Donatello), and
the others, Nencio (Ghiberti), Luca (della Robbia) and
Masaccio, were inspired in each of your famous works by
that genius to which the artists of antiquity also owe their
fame."

All the artists quoted not only had the study of antiquity
in common, by which means they hoped to find the ideal
proportion, but they were also personally closely connected.
They knew each other, were friends and worked together.
This mutual inspiration and the interaction of architecture,
painting and sculpture played a fundamental role in the
development of the artistic style which the biographer of
the artists, architect and artist himself, Giorgio Vasari
(1511–1574), called the "buona maniera moderna" a
hundred years after it came into existence.

Alberti places Brunelleschi in first place; his importance
as an architect was evident in a series of major buildings.
Thus the dome of the cathedral, for example, mirrors
the new feeling for form which entered ecclesiastical
architecture with Brunelleschi. Donatello, the most famous
sculptor of the Florentine early Renaissance next to Ghiberti,
was publicly represented with his sculptures at many sites
in the city, while Ghiberti was just working on the second
door of the Florentine Baptistery, the famous Paradise door.
Masaccio was honored posthumously after his early death
in 1428, having left posterity significant works in the

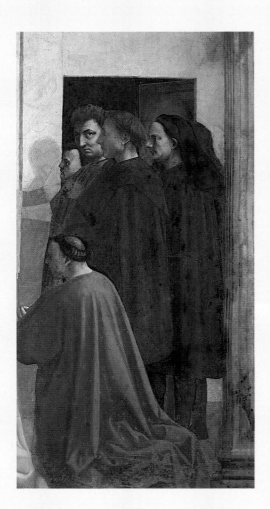

unusual frescoes, conceived with perspective in mind, in the Brancacci Chapel and Santa Maria Novella. Alberti presumably knew early works of della Robbia – whose sculptures were later to combine in ideal form with Brunelleschi's architecture and who helped clay sculpture to new fame – since his first main work, the marble singer's gallery for the cathedral had not yet been completed at the time that the treatise on painting was written.

In fine art there is little pictorial evidence, often subject to various interpretations, to give an impression of who were thought to be the greatest artists of the time by their contemporaries.

This includes Masaccio's fresco *Raising of the Son of Theophilus and St Peter Enthroned* in Santa Maria del Carmine (ill. 7), which was painted some years before the publication of Alberti's treatise on painting in 1428. Next to the biblical scene to the left of St Peter on his throne, a group of four men is attending the event; these are thought to be portraits, from left to right, of Masolino, Masaccio, Alberti and Brunelleschi.

A painting in the Louvre, dated from between 1500 and 1565, is linked with one of the achievements of the early Renaissance, the discovery of perspective. It shows Brunelleschi in a group with four other famous men, the *Fathers of Perspective* (ill. 6). An inscription, which was added later, names these figures depicted in a row of frieze-like busts. Together with Giotto – the first artist to have loosened the bonds of the Byzantine tradition, who thus stood at the start of the development of modern painting

– artists and scientists are depicted who contributed their knowledge of perspective, gained by intensive study, to the modernization of fine art: Paolo Uccello, Donatello, the mathematician and biographer Antonio Manetti and Brunelleschi.

Giorgio Vasari writes about this painting in his *Vita* of Paolo Uccello, to whom he ascribes the work, as follows: "The first one was Giotto, for illuminating and rejuvenating art, the second Filippo di Ser Brunellesco for architecture, the third Donatello for sculpture, then he depicted himself for perspective (…), and finally, for mathematics, Giovanni Manetti, his friend, with whom he frequently discussed matters and spoke about Euclid's theories."

THE COMPETITION FOR THE BAPTISTERY DOOR

In gratitude for the end of the plague which had struck Florence in 1400, the Signoria, the council of the city, pledged to decorate the Baptistery of San Giovanni with bronze doors. A competition was announced in 1401 in which seven artists took part, including Lorenzo Ghiberti and Filippo Brunelleschi. The participants were instructed to illustrate the story of the sacrifice of Isaac. The Gothic quatrefoil was specified as the shape of the frame.

It was necessary to specify this form, consisting of four rounded stylized leaves, to accord with the bronze reliefs of the first Baptistery door by Andrea Pisano (1295–1395) which were created from 1330 onwards. The subject was well chosen. It made it easy for the judges to assess whether the competitors were able to combine a composition with multiple interacting figures with a landscape perspective.

Of the bronze reliefs which were executed, only the two by Ghiberti and Brunelleschi have been preserved. A comparison of the two works (ills. 9, 10) has in the meantime become an almost classical theme in art historiography. Both artists have their supporters. This is hardly surprising, given that this is thought to represent the birth of the Renaissance – and not only from the perspective of art history. The very fact that a competition was announced represents a change in the way that art was perceived and also a change in attitude towards artists. It is equally significant that we know about the progress of the competition from reports by Ghiberti and Manetti.

Antonio Manetti, Brunelleschi's biographer, wrote about his design: "All were surprised by the 'difficulties' he had set himself – Abraham's pose, his thumb placed under Isaac's chin, the action in his movement, his garment and his attitude; the delicate nature of Isaac the boy; the posture and clothing of the angel, his attitude and the way in which he reaches for Abraham's hand (ill. 8); and the pose and attitude and delicateness of the man who is pulling a thorn out of his foot (ill. 11), and of the other man who is bending forward to drink (ill. 12). They were surprised by the 'difficulties' which these figures contain and how well they perform their functions." Here Filippo Brunelleschi is characterized as an artist who loves difficulties. This represents praise in

terms of the Renaissance perception of art. To overcome difficult tasks was proof of talent and technical skill; the good artist solved problems with ease.

What elements do Brunelleschi's relief and Ghiberti's have in common, and where do their differences lie? Both works contain all the figures which are named in the Bible. Ghiberti places them along a diagonal line which runs from bottom left to top right; the action of the picture must be read like a line of writing. Brunelleschi, in contrast, inserts all figures – with the significant exception of the angel – into a triangular composition. The two subordinate figures, which form the corner points of the base, extend beyond the frame, while the tip is taken by father and son. This difference in construction shows clearly that Brunelleschi arranges a more dramatic staging of the story. The angel can only just prevent Abraham from killing Isaac by his intervention.

Classical references are found in both works. Ghiberti's Isaac reproduces a classical nude, Brunelleschi worked the "man pulling out a thorn", the Roman copy of a work from the third century BC, into his composition. The latter is a completely unbiblical figure, while the nude ennobles the figure of Isaac.

The jury, which included Giovanni di Bicci de' Medici – who was to play an important role in Brunelleschi's life – chose Ghiberti as the winner of the competition. That his work was more in line with the international softness of style, was less bold in other words, was probably not the only factor to have played a part in the decision. Purely economic aspects may also have been decisive. Ghiberti obviously required less bronze for his relief and he cast it in one piece, while Brunelleschi fixed the individual figures to a prepared base. One can see from the figures that each one was individually cast – and should also be studied in its own right. But this dissolves the unity of the whole into its component parts.

Brunelleschi drew the consequences from his defeat and henceforth turned to other tasks. There is no evidence of further sculptural work by him from the mid-1420's onwards at the latest. He never came to terms with this setback, if his biographers are to be believed.

9, 10 Filippo Brunelleschi and Lorenzo Ghiberti
The Sacrifice of Isaac, 1401
Gilded bronze, 45 x 38 cm
Museo Nazionale del Bargello, Florence

Both reliefs combine the *dramatis personae* which belong to the narrative: the two servants and the donkey, Abraham and Isaac, the angel and the ram. Ghiberti adheres more closely to the Bible text, which says among other things that the ram is behind Abraham and that the angel only calls out to him but does not actually intervene in the events. The liberty which Brunelleschi takes benefits the increased drama of the action.

17

The two servants have adopted novel stances; Brunelleschi demonstrates the sovereign way in which he is able to make bodies appear from unexpected angles. The contrast to the way Ghiberti's figures are developed could not be more striking. These are, furthermore, figures which do not fit into the framework. It is as if they have been imposed on the Gothic quatrefoil.

The bronze relief had been preceded by works for the silver altar in the cathedral of Pistoia (ills. 13, 14). These date from about 1399/1400. The half-figures of the prophets Jeremiah and Isaiah, a sitting figure of the Evangelist and the full figure of St. Augustine are ascribed to Brunelleschi. In addition, we know that Brunelleschi made a wooden crucifix (ill. 15) which, according to an anecdote told by Vasari, has its origins in a competition with Donatello. The wooden cross is dated to between 1410 and 1425. The Christ figure is developed on a 170 x170 cm square. It is based on the modular pattern of the *homo quadratus* by Vitruvius.

This is worth noting, as the ground plans of the basilicas of *San Lorenzo* and *Santo Spirito* are also based on the human figure so that here we can see a significant anticipation of Brunelleschi's architectural work: Christ as prefiguration of the house of God.

The value which Brunelleschi himself placed on his bronze relief may be seen in the fact that he had it mounted clearly visible for everyone to see in his oldest completed building, the *Old Sacristy*. For Ghiberti, his victory marked the start of a career without precedent. For both it was their first competition against one another. It was not their last.

13, 14 (below and right) *Evangelist* and *St. Augustine,* 1399/1400
Bronze, height 19.5 and 23.3 cm
Silver altar of St. Jacob, San Zeno, Pistoia

Both these works belong to Brunelleschi's early works, the oldest
which have been preserved. The high reliefs of two prophets, a
sitting figure of the Evangelist and the standing figure of St.
Augustine, are ascribed to him. These works give little indication of
Brunelleschi's future capacities in composition, which were
demonstrated shortly thereafter in the relief of *The Sacrifice of Isaac.*

15 *Crucifix,* between 1410 and 1425
Wood, 170 x 170 cm
Santa Maria Novella, Cappella Gondi, Florence

In his biography of Donatello, Giorgio Vasari informs us of the
origin of this work. When Donatello showed his friend a cross
which he had created, Brunelleschi answered: "It seems to me that
you have fixed a peasant to your cross." This caused Donatello to
challenge Brunelleschi to do it better. When he saw the resulting
work, Donatello was frank enough to admit: "You have been
granted the ability to depict the Savior, I to depict peasants."

THE DISCOVERY OF CENTRALIZED PERSPECTIVE

Brunelleschi's buildings mark the start of Renaissance architecture. But it appears that we owe this artist a further invention which defined art for centuries: the discovery of centralized perspective. It possibly represents "the theoretically most innovative moment in all of Brunelleschi's interests" (Pizzigoni). In his biography, Vasari writes: "Filippo occupied himself a great deal with perspective, of which there was little experience at the time and in which many things were carried out wrongly. He spent much of his time in the study of this subject until he found a completely correct method, namely one which is based on the ground plan and profile and uses intersecting lines (ill. 17), a truly useful matter which benefits the art of drawing and which caused Filippo such pleasure that he made a drawing of the square of San Giovanni (ill. 18) with all the sections of the black and white marble squares at the church. The parts which are furthest away recede in a very dainty manner. In the same way he represented the building of the Misericordia including the stalls of the wafer-makers and the vault of the Pecori and on the other side the pillar of St. Zenobius. Much praised by artists and all those who are able to judge art, this work encouraged him soon afterwards to compose a view of the palace, the market, the loggia of the Signoria (ill. 19) and the roof of the Pisani, including all the other buildings in the vicinity. This drawing aroused the interest of other artists who immediately pursued such studies with great enthusiasm."

Brunelleschi's biographer Manetti also refers to the two perspective views of the Baptistery and the Piazza della Signoria; indeed, he claims to have held them in his hands on several occasions and thus to be able to "verify" their existence. The two drawings have unfortunately been lost. It is possible that they were in the possession of Lorenzo de' Medici, something which would show the enormous regard in which they were held.

Manetti also gives us a definition of perspective. He writes: "What painters currently call perspective is that part of the science of perspective which in practice results in the good and systematic reduction or increase in size, as it appears to the human eye, of objects, be they distant or within reach – of buildings, plains, mountains or landscapes of every kind, and of figures and other

things at every point – to the size which they seem to have from a distance, depending how near or far away they are."

The reference to science is a point worth noting. Nothing is quite as characteristic of 15th century artists – and, as a consequence, of the change of emphasis in their training – as theory. Increasingly they sought to understand the structure of their works, the processes and techniques of their art, the conditions of their creativity, through experiment, but also through reflection. In this they found support in humanist circles and through classical authorities whose writings were being rediscovered. For architecture this was primarily Vitruvius. In the last but one decade of the first century BC, the classical author Lucius Vitruvius Mammora, also known as Marcus Vitruvius Pollio, wrote his work "De architectura", "On architecture". This comprehensive and systematic treatise on the building profession has, if we look at its reception, become the most successful text on architecture. Only by becoming a theoretician does the craftsman emancipate himself and turn into an artist. For it is at this point, when he is seen not as a secondary creator, a mere imitator of nature for example, but as a primary creator who manages to surpass nature, that he becomes equal in rank to the scholar – and the theologian. The *divina artista*, the "divine artist" of the Renaissance, makes his first appearance. The tracts and treatises of Leon Battista Alberti (1404–1472), Piero della Francesca (ca.1420–1492) or Leonardo da Vinci (1452–1519) demonstrate that theoretical reflection had become just as much a part both of their work as of their perception of themselves as artists.

The classical period, which proved such a model for the Renaissance, was not, however, familiar with the laws by which things grow smaller as they recede into the distance. "No classical artist would have been able to draw the famous avenue of poplars which leads into the picture until it disappears on the horizon." (Gombrich). Brunelleschi was the first to give his contemporaries the tools by which they could solve this problem, and since he made use of scientific disciplines such as geometry and optics, each picture constructed using the laws of perspective could henceforth be taken to be the result of a scientific way of working. Both Manetti and Vasari

date the artist's experiments with perspective to the early period. Today it is agreed that they fall into the second decade of the 15th century, between 1415 and 1420. The answer to the question as to how Brunelleschi arrived at his views on perspective remains the subject of controversy. Various attempts have been made to reconstruct them. With the Baptistery panel, to which Manetti expressly refers, he might in the first instance have stretched a network of threads over the reveal of the cathedral portal in order then to place a plate with an eye-level hole at a certain distance. Then he "scanned" the Baptistery with the aid of the eye-level hole square by square, as it were, using the network of threads. To draw the "picture" created in this way, Brunelleschi used a square panel on which the patterns of thread squares had been reproduced to scale but reduced in size. Then he transferred the points and lines of the network of squares into the relevant square of the panel.

The possible correctness of this assumption is supported by the fact that Leon Battista Alberti, who wrote down the first, slightly modified, instructions

for this procedure, dedicated his treatise "Della pittura libri tre", "Three books on painting", to Brunelleschi in 1436. Based on Brunelleschi, Alberti supplies the first instructions for constructing a painting using centralized perspective (ill. 20). According to him, the conditions under which perspective is of use in a spatial representation require not only that all the objects are shown as receding, but that the whole picture turns into a window (ill. 16) through which we imagine that we are looking into the space. This means that the real base on which the picture is created, be it a painting or relief surface, is neutralized to become a mere image base onto which a complete space is projected, containing all the individual objects seen through the surface. This projection in turn is based on the proper geometrical construction. Using the window definition, we might imagine it as follows: the picture represents a plane section of the sight pyramid – Alberti refers to a "intersegazione della piramide visiva". This is created by treating the visual center as a point which is connected with the individual characteristic points of the space to

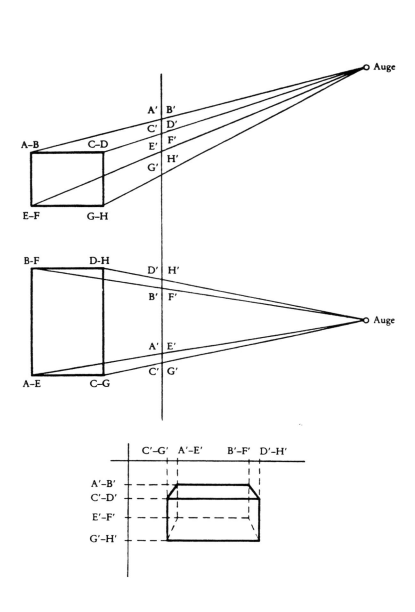

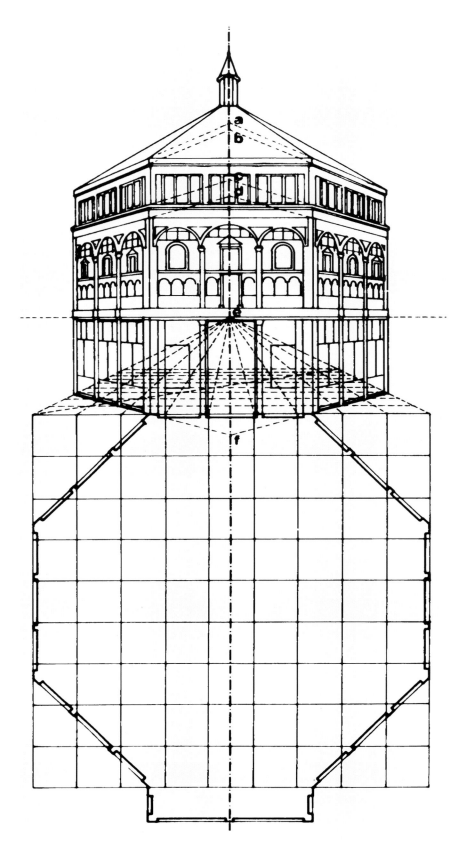

17 Construction in perspective of a block by means of the *construzione legittima*, a combination of ground plan and elevation which is thought to have been invented by Brunelleschi between 1415 and 1420

As an architect, Brunelleschi was used to thinking in these terms. In the two preparatory drawings, the sight pyramid is represented by triangles which have their apex at the point which represents the eye. The picture plane which intersects the sight pyramid describes a vertical plane. In the ground plan the objects appear as a horizontal diagram, in elevation, in contrast, as a vertical one. The picture in perspective itself is created by combining the two drawings in a third.

18 Schematic reconstruction of Brunelleschi's first panel with a view of the Baptistery of San Giovanni, Florence, in centralized perspective (according to Parronchi)

It is no coincidence that Brunelleschi chose the Baptistery to demonstrate his experiment. In drawing, the geometrical patterns of the building almost demand the discovery of the laws of perspective.

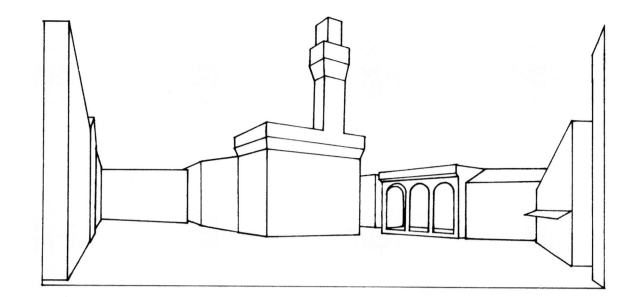

19 Schematic reconstruction of Brunelleschi's second panel with a view of the Piazza della Signoria with the Palazzo Vecchio, Florence, in centralized perspective (according to Ragghianti)

There have been various reconstruction attempts as the two panels by Brunelleschi have not been preserved, and we thus do not know what they looked like.

20 Construction in perspective of the 'basic square' with its chess board-like divisions (according to Alberti)

Around 1435, Leon Battista Alberti started not with the ground plan and elevation as Brunelleschi had done, "but with the organization in perspective of the representation itself" (Panofsky). In a preparatory drawing he divides the base line of a picture square into equal parts (a to b) and adds a centralized vanishing point (A). A "pencil of rays" is created if the latter point is combined with the former. Then the correct distance of the diagonal lines must be determined with mathematical accuracy. Alberti resorts to Brunelleschi for this, to the elevation of the sight pyramid – originally carried out on a separate sheet – which shows the points of intersection of the diagonal lines (v to z) on a vertical line which is identical with the side of the picture square.

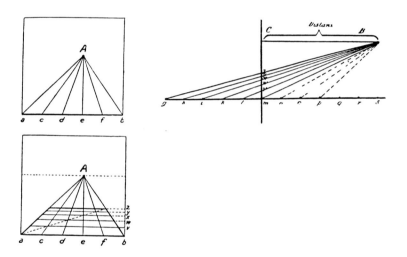

be depicted. In the picture which is thus produced, all orthogonals or depth lines meet at the sight point; parallel lines, in whichever direction they go, have a common vanishing point; equal dimensions are progressively reduced the further back they are, in such a way that each section can be calculated from its preceding or succeeding one. This leads to the "creation of a completely rational, i.e. infinite, constant and homogenous space" (Panofsky). The importance of this discovery by Brunelleschi cannot be overestimated. Two concluding references may illustrate the point. It is reported of the Florentine painter Paolo Uccello (1397–1475), who was one generation younger than Brunelleschi and truly obsessed by perspective, that he answered his wife when she urged him finally to come to bed: "Perspective is the sweetest thing". A century later, the great Leonardo da Vinci described it as the "helm and connecting thread of painting". These remarks allow us to gauge how this discovery was viewed. It was to remain so for centuries. Not until the end of the 19th century did artists such as van Gogh or Cézanne emancipate themselves from the overpowering role which perspective had acquired as an element of construction.

22 (opposite) Tommaso di Ser Giovanni Cassai,
known as Masaccio
The Holy Trinity, ca. 1425–1427
Fresco, 667 x 317 cm
Santa Maria Novella, Florence

The architecture of the chapel shows Brunelleschi's
classical language of forms; their laws of centralized
perspective are used here for the first time. The chapel
and sarcophagus have a common vanishing point which
lies at the eye-level of the observer. This cooperation
between painter and architect makes *The Holy Trinity* into
one of the earliest examples of the new painting.

21 (below) *Masaccio's Imaginary Chapel of the Holy
Trinity*, reconstruction of the architectural structure
(according to Sampaolesi)

Reconstruction of the architectural structure (left) and the
spatial dimensions (right) for *Masaccio's Imaginary Chapel
of the Holy Trinity*. The drawing shows us the size we are
to imagine the chapel. It is four and a half meters in
length and two and a half at its widest point. Masaccio's
fresco thus opens a room of approximately 9 to 11 square
meters. In order to have a perfect view of the illusion
contained in the painting, the work must be looked at
from a distance greater than five meters.

It is thought that Masaccio's *The Holy Trinity* was created
between 1425 and 1427 (ill. 22). We do not know the exact
date because the relevant documents are missing. But this
fresco represents a stroke of genius for the young artist,
born in 1401, whose real name was Tommaso di Ser
Giovanni Cassai. The wall painting, 667 x 317 cm, has at its
center the motif of the throne of grace, that is, God the
Father on his throne holding the cross with Christ in both
hands. The Holy Spirit is present in the form of a dove. Mary
and John, whom we encounter in representations of the
crucifixion but not of the throne of grace, stand on either
side of the Trinity. The donors appear kneeling on a ledge,
but in contrast to the medieval tradition their figures are the
same size as those of the biblical figures. The lower part of
the fresco shows a skeleton lying on a sarcophagus; its
meaning is set out in an inscription: "I was what you are;
you will become what I am now."

We know that Masaccio, for whose residence in Florence
there is documentary evidence from 1422 onwards, was a
friend of the much older Brunelleschi. This is why it is
assumed that the architectural framework, and possibly also
the order of the figures in the compositional triangle, go
back to the latter. The way in which the figures and the
architecture are put in a coherent spatial relationship is
remarkable. The fresco was created in 24 "days of work".
With a real fresco, the so-called *buon fresco*, the artist paints
on the damp plaster so that the paint combines with it as
it dries. The painter therefore only applies as much plaster
as he can work on. This gives rise to the "days of work".

During the first ten, Masaccio designed the architecture: the
two fluted pilasters and the Corinthian capitals, the
architrave, the pillars with the Ionic capitals and the panelled
barrel vault.

According to traditional iconography in painting, such
classical building forms are not part of either the motif of
the throne of grace or the crucifixion. With the former,
we would expect a gold background as an indication of
its sacred nature. Instead, we see here "the greatest
conscientiousness in the reproduction of natural forms,
clarity of geometrical structure and the insignia of the
classical architectural alphabet" (Braunfels). The latter two
points may be related directly to Brunelleschi. In his
Barbadori Chapel, started in approximately 1419 but
unfortunately altered a great deal in the 16th and 18th
centuries, he first formulated this architectural language:
the supporting pillars with the Corinthian capitals and
the half-pillars leaning against them. "The surprise of the
people of Florence must have been great when this fresco
was unveiled, simulating a hole in the wall through which
they looked into a new chapel in Brunelleschi's modern
building style." (Gombrich).

That surprise has lasted to the present day. The structure
of the picture with its complete centralized perspective
makes it possible to reconstruct the architectural design of
the depicted chapel and to determine the position of the
figures within it (ill. 21). This masterful handling of the rules
of perspective was a rare event at the time and certainly not
commonplace.

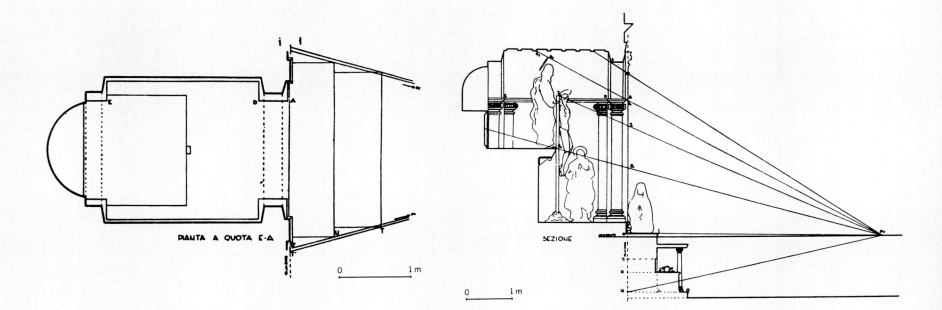

PIANTA A QUOTA E-A   0   1 m

SEZIONE   0   1 m

The Ospedale degli Innocenti

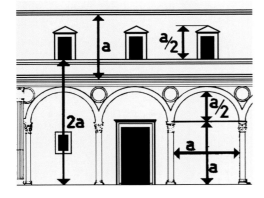

23 *Ospedale degli Innocenti*, relationships of proportion of the façade (according to De Angelis D'Ossat)

This diagrammatic representation shows more clearly the relationships of proportion which determine the harmony of the façade. The basic measure (a) corresponds to the distance between two pillars; it is 10 Florentine cubits (5.84 m).

24 *Ospedale degli Innocenti*, façade (detail ill. 29), 1419–1427

Brunelleschi may have taken the idea for the aedicule windows which rest on the cornice from the Baptistery façade. Both the architrave and the spandrel have bands lying above one another which project slightly from bottom to top. These are fasciae. They belong to the classical order; there are usually three of them, and more rarely two. The so-called "Infants" were put into the spandrels in 1487, terracotta medallions by Andrea della Robbia. They are a visible indication of the Ospedale's function: a house for foundlings.

The *Ospedale degli Innocenti* (ill. 29, cf. also ill. 25), the Foundling Hospital, was intended as a home for orphans. It is "the building in which the Renaissance style appears for the first time" (Pevsner).

We know from architectural history that the Brunelleschi began work on the Ospedale in 1419 on instructions from the Silk Merchants, the Arte della Seta. His presence on the building site is documented from the beginning. He supervised construction until 1427 but from 1423 onwards he appears to have been present less and less. Brunelleschi was succeeded as architect and master builder by Francesco della Luna. The foundling hospital was inaugurated in 1445. This is one of Brunelleschi's first buildings and we can already observe a characteristic which applies to most of the others. The artist never completed them – as he never completed the Ospedale – and his successors often changed and distorted the original design.

Since the work on the Ospedale has been thoroughly documented, like the work on the cathedral dome, we are able to separate Brunelleschi's work very clearly from that of della Luna. In this respect Antonio Manetti's writings are a help; he criticizes della Luna harshly. According to these documents, the lower part of the building had already been built when Brunelleschi left in 1427: a ninefold arcade of arches with a pilaster field on either side through which a small portal led to the interior. Brunelleschi did not write any architectural treatises but the tendency towards an architectural canon can be read from his building works and their elements. He preferred Corinthian capitals (ill. 28), which retain the form he established in the Ospedale *portico*, throughout all of his work. The extent to which Brunelleschi's regulated view of architecture contrasted with that of his contemporaries is illustrated by the following. The concept of *varietas*, variety, which almost becomes the hallmark of the Renaissance "style" originates with Alberti. The architect who responded to this call for variety as did no other is Michelozzo (1396–1472). In his tabernacle in San Miniato al Monte we find four different capitals next to one another. Brunelleschi, by comparison, is restrained almost to the point of asceticism. In his two basilicas, San Lorenzo and Santo Spirito, there is but a single

form, the Corinthian capital, which is found on the free-standing pillars and the wall pillars, the wall pilasters and the crossing pilasters (ills. 33, 40). The arch over round pillars is one of Brunelleschi main motifs and also one which he introduced to Renaissance architecture. Despite Alberti's rejection, the use of pillar and arch in combination becomes a firm part of the vocabulary of the language of architecture. In his treatise "De re aedificatoria" ("Of architecture"), which appeared in 1485, Alberti demands that pillars should be topped by entablatures instead of arches and notes that arches should be supported by *columnae quadrangulae*, by columns. As a consequence there is no combination of the two building elements by this architect and theoretician.

The changes which della Luna made to the façade of the Ospedale, the core of the building complex, may be summarized in three points. Brunelleschi had planned to conclude the loggia on either the side with one pilaster field each. By adding a second one on the right, his successor broke the intended symmetry. In addition, della Luna had the architrave on the outer pilasters broken up and extended down to the plinth (ill. 26), thereby creating a frame for the lower field of the façade. It is easy to discover the model which inspired the architect. It is the attic field of the Baptistery (ill. 27). Manetti reports that della Luna had probably expected to be praised by Brunelleschi for this idea. When the latter inspected the changes to his building after a longer absence he did not, however, see them as an improvement. Giorgio Vasari, who embellishes Manetti's description somewhat, has Brunelleschi say that della Luna had copied the only mistake contained in the Baptistery. This episode reveals a great deal about Brunelleschi's view of architecture. That he does not regard the descending architrave of the upper Baptistery story as exemplary illustrates Brunelleschi's critical faculties, even in relation to a building which in his time was still considered to be classical and which thus served as an unquestioned model. The Baptistery was thought to be a Roman temple which had been transformed into a Christian church. In Brunelleschi's architectural system the architrave is no longer a framework motif but a horizontal part of the building. In this way he

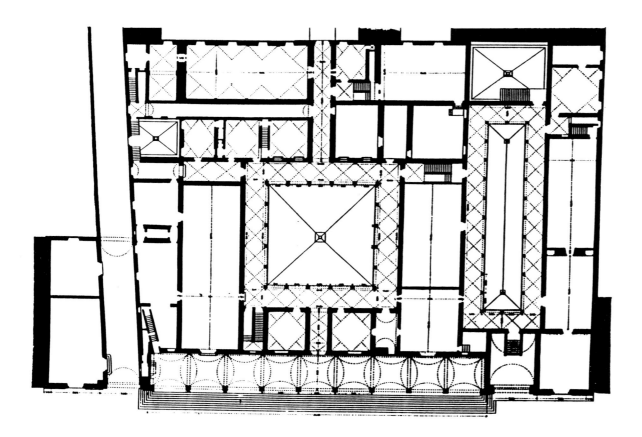

25 *Ospedale degli Innocenti,* ground plan

The view of the complex as a whole shows the small size of the portico in relation to the whole building. It nevertheless dominates the side from which it is seen, where the main entrance is situated.

confronts the medieval ambiguity, which still allowed for both interpretations, with his clear rules. While the first two interventions date from the period around 1430, the third dates from the end of the 1430s. It relates to the upper storey, the roof cornicing of which is not sufficiently developed and in which the two pilasters are missing which should have separated the outer windows from the central façade. These wall pillars would have provided a continuation of those from the lower storey. Even if we were not aware of the original plan, the shape of the façade would draw our attention to this error. The concluding pilaster fields are a little wider than the open arcades, which sets the two outer windows on the right and the left apart from the inner ones: "This hardly noticeable difference in dimension would be justified by a pilaster framework reserved exclusively for the outer fields." (Klotz).

Despite della Luna's intervention, it is still evident today how well-proportioned the organization of the façade of the Ospedale is (ills. 23, 29). The ground floor consists of an open arcade, its slim pillars and wide arches opening out this part of the building. The upper storey has small rectangular windows with a pediment which sits above the vertex of the arches. The rhythm from below continues above in this way. A stepped architrave separates the two storeys. Colored terracotta medallions by Andrea della Robbia (1435–1525) can be seen in the spandrels of the arches, the so-called "Infants", which were put up in 1485 (ill. 24). Despite the popularity today of these medallions, which give an indication of the purpose of the building, they did not accord with Brunelleschi's intentions. If it had been up to the architect, the medallions would have remained

empty. Their effect would then have been similar to the one which is familiar to us from Masaccio's architecture in the fresco of *The Holy Trinity* (ill. 22). As an architect, Brunelleschi was a purist.

The measure on which the proportions of the Ospedale are based is the clear distance between two pillars (ill. 31). This is based on the classical theoretician Vitruvius and in this case determines the height of the pillars as well as the distance from the architrave to the cornice of the upper storey; the height of the windows including the pediment and radius, the height of the arch, corresponds to half the measure. The double measure, in turn, is given by the height of the façade from the resting place at the base to the cornice on which the windows rest.

Although the aedicule frames of the windows and the Corinthian pillars represent classical motifs, Brunelleschi's loggia is distinguished from classical buildings such as the Colosseum in Rome by its slender pillars and the width of the bays. Thus it is the architecture of the proto-Renaissance from the 11th and 12th centuries – the Baptistery in Florence, above all – which has tended to be used as a model; the origin of the shape of the windows may be found here.

Also, we must not forget that the ospedale loggia already existed in the 14th century, such as the Ospedale di San Matteo (about 1390) in Florence or the Ospedale (1406) in Lastra a Signa. The elevation of these hospitals is similar to Brunelleschi's: a two storey façade is divided into a loggia and a row of windows above it. Brunelleschi's loggia is distinguished from the earlier ones by the slim monolithic pillars whose shafts consist of one piece, the moldings on the spandrels of the arches,

26, 27 (top) *Ospedale degli Innocenti,* detail of the façade (top) compared with the attic field with "breaking" architrave in the Baptistery of San Giovanni, 1059–1150 (above)

The view of the model and copy side by side makes the justification of Brunelleschi's criticism particularly clear. The architrave "breaking" into the vertical direction, although it should be a load-bearing element of the impost, "degenerates" into a form of ornamentation.

28 *Ospedale degli Innocenti,* façade (detail: a capital)

The form of capital which Brunelleschi uses here takes on a composite character due to the egg and dart between the volutes and the abacus slab. The size of the volutes is later reduced, something which is already indicated in the pilaster capitals of the Foundling Hospital.

29 *Ospedale degli Innocenti*, façade, construction started 1419,
directed by Brunelleschi until 1427
Piazza SS. Annunziata, Florence

The side on view is clearly structured: an open arcade with pillars
and arches below, windows with pediments above. These are
positioned above the vertex of the arches and thus continue the
rhythm of the lower storey. The two storeys are divided by an
architrave. A flight of stairs – as in a Roman temple – leads up to
the porch.

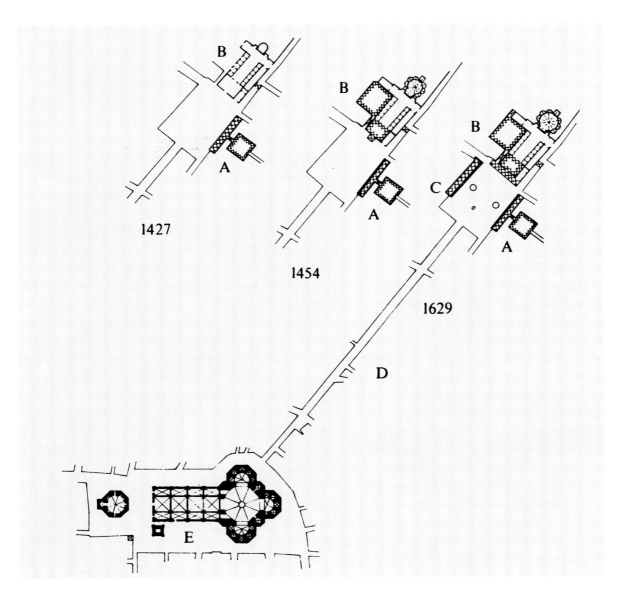

1427

1454

1629

B

A

B

A

C

A

B

A

D

E

30 *Piazza SS. Annunziata,* diagram of the stages of development (according to Bacon)

This diagram illustrates the development of Piazza Santissima Annunziata in the period from the 15th to the 17th century (A = Ospedale degli Innocenti, 1419 ff.; B = Church of Santissima Annunziata with Michelozzo's courtyard, 1444 ff., and the portico, 1601 ff.; C = Portico of Antonio da Sangallo and Baccio D'Agnolo, 1516 ff.) and the linking of the square to Santa Maria del Fiore, the Cathedral (E), by the Via dei Servi (D).

31 *Ospedale degli Innocenti,* façade

View into the arcade with its clear division of space. The pillar, in its slimness and regularity, its fineness and clarity of execution, is encountered here for the first time since classical times "as an architectural allegory of the human being" (Klotz).

and above all the flight of stairs across the whole width which opens the loggia up to the square.

The model nature of Brunelleschi's clear façade structure, and thus its forward-looking character, can be seen in the buildings which make reference to his Ospedale, such as the Loggia di San Paolo at the Piazza Santa Maria Novella in Florence.

Another aspect of the significance of the Ospedale is the way in which it relates to the Piazza SS. Annunziata, the creation of which is closely connected with the construction of the Ospedale. The square was largely derelict land when the loggia of the foundling hospital was built on its east side. The north side was dominated by the façade of the church of Santissima Annunziata. Today the façade lies behind the atrium and the porch, which were added in the 16th century. At the beginning of that century, the loggia was created in the west under Antonio da Sangallo the elder and Baccio d'Agnolo. In its construction and structure it makes direct reference to Brunelleschi's on the opposite side. The square was

concluded to the south in the mid-16th century with the Palazzo Grifoni.

The development of the square is particularly significant in the context of town planning in the 15th and 16th centuries. There are two indications that Brunelleschi already expected the square to have a regular plan. He placed the portico of the Ospedale exactly parallel to the axis of the church and thus provided the alignment for the loggia which was to form the boundary of the square on the other side. Opposite the church of Santissima Annunziata, the Via dei Servi leads into the square. This road axis had been laid down as early as the 14th century; it "points" on the one hand to the façade of the church, and on the other to the cathedral choir. This relationship was not only respected by Brunelleschi, he integrated it into the plans for his building and thereby also laid the foundations for the development of the west side. He initiated the first axis-related site development in the modern era, governed by symmetry and harmony.

SAN LORENZO

It is possible to relate Brunelleschi's churches of *San Lorenzo* and *Santo Spirito* (ills. 33, 40) to one another. Both are spacious, pillared basilicas with a nave and two aisles whose naves, resting on pillars, are wider and higher than the two aisles. The nave and aisles are supplemented by transepts and choir so that the ground plan corresponds to a Latin cross. This church form, which has its origins in early Christian church architecture, was developed in Florence as early as the Romanesque period San Miniato al Monte and St. Apostoli are regarded as the most impressive examples. The nave and transepts of Brunelleschi's basilicas are flat-roofed, the crossing and aisles in contrast are vaulted. Whereas with *San Lorenzo* he had to take into account the existing Romanesque building, as well as certain conditions imposed by building work in progress, above all in the transepts, in *Santo Spirito* he was able to create a church wholly in accordance with his ideas.

In its present form, *San Lorenzo* is a basilica whose construction dates completely from the 15th century. The extent of Brunelleschi's involvement continues to be the subject of debate. We know that the prior of the church, Matteo Dolfini, had the extension of his church in mind rather than a new building when he developed the first designs in 1418 and started to have them built. They were to encompass the transepts with their chapels and an extension of the nave. In about 1421, after Dolfini's death, Giovanni di Bicci de' Medici (1360–1429) commissioned Brunelleschi, who had been working for him on the *Old Sacristy* of *San Lorenzo* since 1419, to undertake a completely new building. He assured the chapter, the clergy belonging to the church, and the chapel donors that he would assume the building costs for the transepts and the nave and aisles. When Brunelleschi began building work on the choir chapels and the transepts he had to include their arrangement in his building design, as a start had already

34 (opposite) *San Lorenzo*, view through the aisles into the chapels

The way in which Brunelleschi relates the individual building sections and forms to one another as elements of his architectural system is clearly evident. The semi-circular arch is repeated several times: in the arcades of the nave, the transverse arches, the arches of the chapel walls. He has managed this despite the fact that he was initially faced with a construction problem. Because the chapels are lower than the aisles – in contrast to Santo Spirito – a wall area remained free above their arches which had to be structured. Brunelleschi inserted the oculi, small round windows, and an entablature. This creates a formal unity between the entrance arches of the chapels and the transverse arches created by the Bohemian caps, as well as being analogous to the nave. The impost bloc at the front, positioned between capital and impost slab, is divided in the same way as the entablature which rests on the pilasters at the back.

35 (right) *San Lorenzo*, the monolithic unfluted pillars of the nave

The use of pillars with classical proportions here instead of columns is a new feature; the former are used as supports in the nave and aisles for the first time in the Renaissance.

been made on the foundations. The western row of chapels had been ordered by Dolfini, who had clearly been prompted to do so by the churches of the mendicant orders in Florence, such as Santa Maria Novella or Santa Croce.

The mendicant orders, which refused all possessions, arose in the 13th century in opposition to the secularization of the Church. Their members, called mendicants, tried to secure their living through work or begging. Committed to a strictly ascetic lifestyle, the mendicant orders saw their task above all in combining monastery life with spiritual and intellectual tasks in daily life. This included pastoral and missionary work,

as well as teaching activities at the universities. The most well known of these orders are the Franciscans, who were responsible for the construction Santa Croce, and the Dominicans with their church of Santa Maria Novella. The row of chapels had an effect on Brunelleschi's architectural system which is still evident today. Vasari already complained about the "limping" pilasters in the interior of the church, referring to the columns in the nave with their associated pilasters on the aisle walls (ill. 34). The latter correspond to the former in their upward reach but are shorter, as a three step flight of stairs leading to the chapels had to be inserted between the bases of the pilasters and the floor.

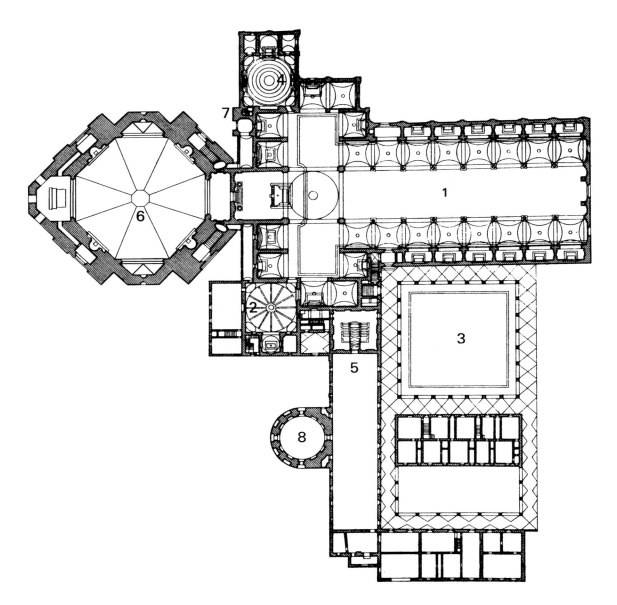

38 (left) *San Lorenzo,* ground plan of the church and monastery

1. Basilica
2. Old Sacristy
3. Cloister (ascribed to Michelozzo, after 1457)
4. New Sacristy (Michelangelo, 1520–1534)
5. Biblioteca Laurenziana (Michelangelo, 1523–1529)
6. Prince's Chapel (Buontalenti and others, 1605–1737)
7. Bell Tower (Ruggieri, 1740–1741)
8. Biblioteca Dolciana (Poccianti, completed 1841).

Building work came to a stop from 1425 to 1442. A very informative document exists, dating from 1434, which was probably written by Brunelleschi himself. Among other things, it provides information about the aisle chapels. According to Manetti, Brunelleschi had planned them from the beginning. But as Giovanni di Bicci found too few donors for them, he had to abandon the idea. At first, therefore, it seemed that the aisles would remain without chapels. But things turned out differently under Giovanni's son Cosimo de' Medici. The latter had probably understood the promise of his father, who died in 1429, to cover the building costs as a firm obligation which he had to meet, including the chapels. Although the document describes the building in all its stages in precise architectural language, the specifications were not followed. The aisle chapels were given a different appearance. According to a ground plan of *San Lorenzo* which Giuliano da Sangallo drew between 1500 and 1512 (ill. 39), the aisle

chapels should also have had a square ground plan with a suspended dome to accord with those in the transepts. But the document of 1434 shows that Brunelleschi had different plans. He intended to construct the chapels as semi-circular conches which would have blended harmoniously with the course of the wall – as he later did successfully in *Santo Spirito*. The chapels were finally built with a transverse rectangular ground plan and barrel vaults. Construction on the nave and aisles did not begin until 1450, four years after Brunelleschi's death. It was concluded in 1494. Brunelleschi was succeeded by Antonio Manetti Ciaccheri, his preferred carpenter for the wooden models. He is responsible for many changes but it is not always clear what they were. As *Santo Spirito* is not only a repetition, but also a continuation of the idea behind the construction of *San Lorenzo,* it is well worthwhile comparing the two churches (cf. ills. 38, 43).

39 (opposite) Giuliano da Sangallo
Ground plan of *San Lorenzo,* between 1500 and 1512
Taccuino di Giuliano da Sangallo, fol. 21 v
Biblioteca Comunale, Siena

According to this ground plan, the chapels above all should have had a different shape from that which they have today: a square ground plan instead of a transverse rectangular one, suspended domes instead of barrel vaults.

SANTO SPIRITO

40 *Santo Spirito*, view of the nave with the 17th century tabernacle

The unit of measurement which governs the ground plan returns in the elevation. At 44 Florentine cubits (25.69 m), the nave is twice as high as it is wide, while the arcade zone and the clerestory, the upper wall section of the basilica lit by the clerestory windows, are of the same height, 22 Florentine cubits (12.84 m). This corresponds to one side of the crossing square. Brunelleschi probably planned a barrel vault instead of the flat ceiling which was to have provided a harmonious finish to the upward elevation.

Brunelleschi started on the plans for this church in 1434. Twelve years passed before construction began. The first pillars for the building were delivered in 1446, ten days before his death. The façade, which was altered in the 18th century, was built in 1482. Despite this, *Santo Spirito* represents the purest example of Brunelleschi's architectural ideas: a building of "ideal logic and cohesion" (Paatz).

The ground plan (ill. 43) shows that the nave, the transepts, the choir and the crossing are exactly equivalent squares. In the nave we find this square four and a half times. The width of the aisles in the transepts and the nave corresponds exactly to half one side of this square. The distance between the pillars is also half the square. The unit of the aisles thus in turn represents a square which is one quarter the size of the large square measure. It occurs 36 times. With the exception of the west end, where special conditions apply, it occurs around the whole of the church building. The ground plan displays a unity which simultaneously forms the measure of the nave and the transepts. As with the *Ospedale degli Innocenti*, this is the distance from one pillar to the next; that is to say, the basic distance between the pillars applies as the square unit for the aisles, and double the distance as the unit for the nave. The proportions of the ground plan, the relationship between the large and small units, can thus be expressed in a numerical relationship of one to four. The small discrepancies which may nevertheless be found can be ignored here. They apply to the crossing and the associated chapels.

The unit of measure in *San Lorenzo* (ill. 38) is not exact because the unit of the nave is not a square. The small aisle unit, on the other hand, is, and its measure forms half the width of the nave. Although the relationship of the units comes close to that of *Santo Spirito*, there is no mathematically exact order.

As the ground plan of *Santo Spirito* has been executed so consistently, it is particularly noticeable that the square measure in the nave can be applied four and a half times. Why not five times? It is tempting to assume a divergence from Brunelleschi's original plan. A ground plan of the church dating from 1465, which we owe to Giuliano da Sangallo, shows a different shape for the

church (ill. 44). It may have been based on a model by Brunelleschi. The aisles and the chapels were clearly intended to carry on round the entrance side of the nave. As a result the faithful would have entered the church through four doors. They would have been received by the chapel-like anterooms and a sort of porch in the form of the aisle. In view of this "radical formal conception", are the aisles still really aisles any more? Have they not been replaced by a sort of "perimeter of space" (Paatz)? What Brunelleschi had planned here was equivalent to "the abandonment of a hitherto almost inviolable tradition of sacred building" (Pevsner). As a result, things turned out differently. In 1482, the plan for the façade of *Santo Spirito* by Salvi d'Andrea, Brunelleschi's successor as architect and master builder, was adopted. The portal was given only three doors. Despite the support of Giuliano da Sangallo, who even turned to Lorenzo de' Medici for help, Brunelleschi's bold design had to make way for a more traditional scheme. At least two other changes must also be mentioned here. The nave, which today is flat-roofed, should have had a barrel vault, which we can imagine similar to the paneled vault in Masaccio's fresco. The last noticeable divergence from the original plan concerns the chapels, whose outside fronts should have remained unfaced.

Does the mathematical clarity which characterizes the ground plan of *Santo Spirito* find its equivalent in the interior of the church? The elevation is indeed determined by an equally clear relationship between the parts. Thus the nave (ill. 40) is exactly twice as high as wide and double the width of the aisles (ill. 45), the ground floor and clerestory have the same height, the height of the bays of the aisles is double their width etc. These basic relationships can also be seen in the building forms. The open arcades of the nave are "repeated" in the walls of the aisles (ill. 49). The pillars there are matched by half-pillars here. This means that the aisles lose their separate importance. They are no longer "chambers" added to the nave, but together with it they form a single, sculpted organism, the "limbs and bones of an architectural organism" (Pizzigoni). In *San Lorenzo* the relationships are not nearly as clear; pilasters structure the walls there (ill. 34). The balance of *Santo*

41 *Santo Spirito*, façade

The volutes and pediments are Baroque additions. If Brunelleschi had had his way, the aisles and the ring of chapels would have continued around the entrance side. Santo Spirito would have become "the hitherto most perfect temple of Christianity", as Vasari put it.

42 *Santo Spirito*, northern external view

Since the external fronts of the chapels were later covered, the shape of their ground plan, the conches, is no longer visible today. The interaction between inner and outer intended by Brunelleschi has been lost; his remarkable view of the character of the wall was abandoned.

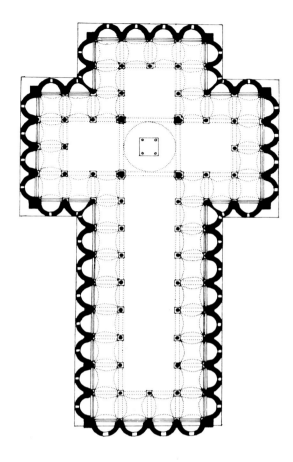

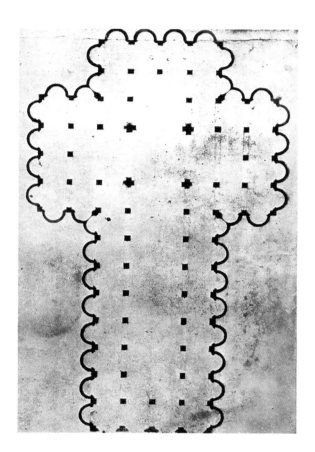

Spirito is due not least to the colors of the church space: the red of the floor, the light gray of the pillars and the white of the wall surfaces.

The relationships of scale and aspects of form outlined above evoke the impression of complete harmony. This impression immediately affects the visitor on entering the church. Brunelleschi's efforts to achieve regular proportions in the ground plan and elevation make him a typical representative of the early Renaissance. Just as his principles of perspective enabled painted space to be structured rationally and logically in painting, so he tried as an architect to clarify the structure of space, to base his buildings on rational and logical relationships.

The bright clarity of *Santo Spirito* also reveals something of the contemporary perception of the world. Gothic other-worldliness makes way for this-worldliness in Renaissance architecture. This developmental tendency is expressed most clearly in the centralized building. The willingness to deal with the reality of this world is not without religious feeling. After all, the cosmos, God's creation, is constructed in

accordance with exact laws and harmonious relationships. People were certain of that at the time. The construction of the east end of *Santo Spirito* marks Brunelleschi's decisive departure from the traditional composition of Romanesque and Gothic churches. The choir and transepts have the same shape, the aisles run round all three building sections at right angles – like a gallery – and the crossing is vaulted by a dome. The model followed by Brunelleschi is close to hand, physically too. It is the church of *Santa Maria del Fiore*, Florence Cathedral. Standing inside *Santo Spirito* and looking east from the nave, one has the impression of being in a centralized building. The centralizing east end is evidence of Brunelleschi's desire to unite a centralized composition, the aesthetic ideal of his time, with the traditional nave and aisles. In the subsequent period, the concept underlying the building of *Santo Spirito* became the ideal of basilica church construction to which others constantly aspired. From da Sangallo via Bramante to Leonardo, it was not only its model character which was important for its reception, but also what it might have been – without the later interventions.

43 (above left) *Santo Spirito*, ground plan, planned ca. 1438
Piazza Santo Spirito, Florence

The ground plan clearly shows the extent to which the building of the church is most thoroughly organized. There is a large unit of measure which governs the nave – based on the crossing square – and a small one which governs the aisles. The latter is defined by the distance between the pillars (11 Florentine cubits = 6.42 m), the former by double the distance (22 Florentine cubits = 12.84 m). Thus four small squares form a large one.

44 (above right) Giuliano da Sangallo
Ground plan of *Santo Spirito*, 1465
Codice Vaticano Latino Barbariniano 4424, fol. 14 v
Biblioteca Apostolica Vaticana, Rome

Da Sangallo's drawing shows the essential aspects of Brunelleschi's design, which were to have characterized the exterior view of the basilica: the ring of chapels which was to have appeared as a series of convex protuberances vaulted to the outside and four instead of the three portals which were built.

45 (opposite) *Santo Spirito*, view of the aisles

In contrast to San Lorenzo, the vaults of the aisles in Santo Spirito are no longer supported by pillars on the one side and pilasters on the other, but exclusively by pillars and half-pillars. Both are of the same height. The half-pillars, which no longer stand on the chapel stairs as the pilasters used to do, but between them, thus no longer "limp". Because of these differences, we now see the aisles as a receding sequence of arches and pillars. This creates an effect of perspective which recalls contemporaneous painting.

46 (below) *Santo Spirito,* detail of the architectural structure: the sequence of pillar bases

The pillars have Attic bases. They consist of a groove between two beadings, of which the top is lower and projects less than the bottom one. This classical form of base was frequently used in Romanesque architecture in the Middle Ages, which is how it might have found its way into Brunelleschi's architectural language.

47 (opposite) *Santo Spirito*, view of one aisle

The sequence "in perspective" of arches and pillars in an aisle.

48 (right) *Santo Spirito*, detail of the architectural structure: a pillar with two arches

The arches and imposts are not decorated, in contrast to San Lorenzo. The ornamental style belongs to Brunelleschi's first basilica, not his second. Since in the latter he executed a unified – no longer an additive – spatial idea, the individual building elements fulfill their function as inter-related elements. As part of a building system with a clearly evident order, such decoration is no longer appropriate.

49 (opposite) *Santo Spirito*, view from the nave through an aisle into the chapels

Since the chapels and aisles in Santo Spirito are of the same height – wholly in keeping with continued development from San Lorenzo – they achieve a different effect. The chapels do not appear as separate independent spaces but as expansions of the wall. They might even be perceived as – enlarged – negative shapes to the flanking half-pillars. The church wall thus projects *and* recedes, it does not have a static effect but one of movement. The windows in the chapel niches contribute to this effect. It is admittedly all the more disruptive that they are partially covered by the high altars which were installed at a later date.

50 (above) *Santo Spirito*, detail of the architectural structure

Solution for the connection between two chapel niches in the corner of the transept.

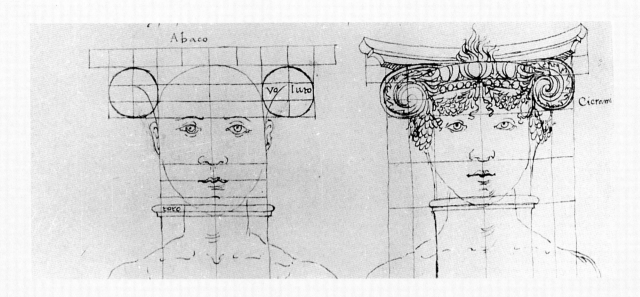

51, 52 Francesco di Giorgio
Pillar and capitals and basilica ground plan with figures
drawn in, after 1482
Pen-and-ink drawings
Biblioteca Reale, Codice Saluzziano 148, fol. 14 v and
fol. 15, Turin
Biblioteca Nazionale, Codice Magliabechiano II. I. 141,
fol. 42 v, Florence

Di Giorgio's drawings in his "Trattati di architettura civile
e militare" illustrate key points of the aesthetics of
Renaissance architecture, namely that there is an analogy
between the pillar and the human figure, between capital
and head, that the construction elements of a basilica are
proportioned as if they were parts of the human body.
According to this, it is the task of the architect to order
the relationship among the parts in such a way that the
building becomes a convincing whole, a body which has
an organic effect, in short, an architectural body. It is to
express the way in which everything corporeal, be it
abstract or organic, in the end reveals one and the same
thing, namely the natural order of all the manifestations
of Creation.

Proportion is of key importance in an architecture which
places such great stress on rational, i. e. regular, clarity.
Clarification of relationships of size becomes the supreme
task of architectural design. If Leon Battista Alberti
(1404–1472) defines the essence of beauty as "the
harmony and agreement of all parts which is achieved
where nothing can be changed, nothing added or taken
away without reducing the perfection of the whole", then
this requirement goes back to the classical theoretician
Vitruvius (first century BC). His theory on architecture, the
text "De architectura", which was rediscovered in 1415, is
"the Bible of the many Renaissance architects and master
builders" (Paatz). Furthermore, Alberti's definition, which
defines Renaissance aesthetics, refers to a fundamental
difference to the Gothic style: the latter embodies in all parts
of its architecture the dynamism of living growth, the
former the unity arising from self-contained building
elements.

We do not know for certain whether or not Brunelleschi
knew the writings of Vitruvius, but we can assume that he
did. Antonio Manetti, his biographer, mentions that he
familiarized himself with proportions and added,
significantly, that this also applied to anatomy. Vitruvius is
the source for the definition of Doric, Ionic and Corinthian
pillars based on the proportions of a man, a woman and a
girl. This translation of human proportions to architecture
expresses the fundamental fact that classical architecture –
in complete contrast to that of the Middle Ages – was
developed in analogy to the proportions of the human body.
Indeed, this correlation is evident from language itself:
capital is derived from the diminutive form of the Latin *caput*
for "head". In the Middle Ages, the proportions of the
pillars could be changed as desired, depending on the
requirements of the functional task they were to perform

in the structure of the building. Not so in the Renaissance.
With a single exception – the *Old Sacristy* which has Ionic
pillars in a subordinate place (lantern balustrade, ill. 62) –
Brunelleschi always uses the Corinthian order.

Given all of these things, it is not surprising that we find
drawings in architectural treatises such as the one by
Francesco di Giorgio (1439–1502) in which a human body
is drawn into the ground plan of a basilica (ill. 52). This
demonstrates in the clearest possible way that the
architectural structure should be understood in analogy to
the human creature.

The harmonious relationships, the proportions in other
words, which make up the compositional structure of a
building are not only expressed in numerical relationships,
for example 1:2 or 2:3, but also through musical concepts;
that is, 1:2 corresponds to the octave, 2:3 to the fifth.
Alberti remarks in this context that "the numbers through
which the harmony of voices appear as something most
beautiful to human beings are the same ones which also fill
the eyes and the soul with wonderful joy". There has been
an unbroken tradition since classical times according to
which music and geometry are fundamentally one: "Music
is the geometry of tones and exactly the same harmonies
on which geometry is based become audible in music."
(Wittkower).

Now both geometry – the theory of spatial relationships –
and music – the science of movement perceived by the ear
– have from ancient times belonged to the quadrivium of
mathematical arts, while architecture – like painting or
sculpture – belongs to the crafts. But if architecture
becomes a mathematical art on the basis of the proportions
it uses, it is raised to the ranks of the liberal arts. To have
executed this transformation is the great achievement of
the 15th century artists.

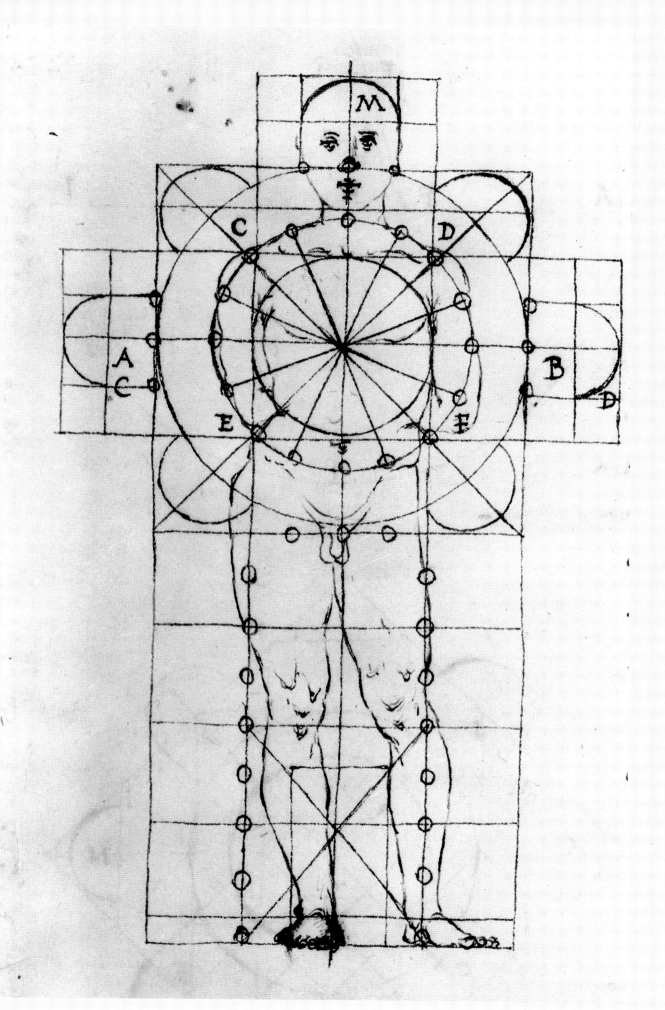

THE OLD SACRISTY

The *Old Sacristy* is the work by Brunelleschi which represents his "architectural debut" (Schedler): a masterpiece of clear proportions and basic geometrical shapes, the perfect example of regular structure.

It was built by Brunelleschi between 1419 and 1429 for use by the Medici as their burial place. Giovanni di Bicci de' Medici, who commissioned the building, and his wife, Riccarda Bueri, as well as two of his grandchildren, sons of Cosimo, found their last resting place here. It is worth noting that this building project was started in competition with another. A little earlier, in 1418, Palla Strozzi had had the sacristy of Santa Trinità built as burial site for his father, Onofrio Strozzi. It is these families, wealthy merchants, "the bankers of Europe" (Pevsner), the Strozzi and the Medici, the Rucellai and the Pitti, who are indivisibly linked with the early Renaissance in Florence through their commissions and in their role as patrons.

Since the end of the 13th century, it had become common for important families to have the rows of chapels in churches turned into burial places for themselves. In this way they created their own memorials. By donating the altar, the chapel was reserved for the individual name "so that the single, 'individualized' chapels became part of the higher unity of the house of God as memorial sites" (Klotz). As the construction of memorials grew in importance, the sacristy was also claimed for this purpose, leading to a change in its function and significance. It was no longer a side chamber of the church – "a preparatory room for the church liturgy, as it were" (Klotz) – in which church vestments and religious objects were kept and where the clergy donned their vestments, but it became a room which had an importance in its own right and which had to meet requirements of status and display. As the sacristy becomes independent, it is clear that, as a side room itself originally, it in turn may have side rooms attached. In the *Old Sacristy* these are the chambers added beside the choir which now take on the character of sacristies. In their interior we find the first barrel vaults of the Renaissance. During the 13th century they were not at all common in Florence. The next stage in this development is not difficult to guess. It is the complete separation from the space of the church. With

Brunelleschi's *Santa Maria degli Angeli* (ill. 79), the family chapel for the descendants of Condottiere Pippo Spano, this stage of emancipation had been completed as far as the construction of memorials was concerned. But there are still more sepulchers by Brunelleschi, for the *Pazzi Chapel* (ill. 68), built as chapter house of the Franciscans of Santa Croce, no longer carries the coat of arms of the order but those of the Pazzi. It is, therefore, also a church space which has been taken over by family memorials.

The interior of the *Old Sacristy* (ill. 53) represents "space of elemental clarity" (Paatz). The main space is a cube with sides eleven and a half meters long on which rests the hemisphere of the umbrella dome. The square substructure is divided into three clearly separated zones: the wall areas, structured by the corner pilasters. The architrave which rests on the latter is followed by semi-circular arches with the pendentives. These two building elements circumscribe the circular form on which the dome rests. The entablature, which runs all the way around, divides the room into two storeys of equal height as well as tying the large space to the smaller altar room since it continues in the latter (ill. 56). This is vaulted in a hemisphere by its dome. Thus Brunelleschi uses a total of three vault forms in the *Old Sacristy*.

The entablature, the great horizontal line, is powerfully contrasted in a vertical direction by the pilasters which strive upwards in the four corners of the main space and at the entrance to the altar room (ill. 53). All arches – be they the wall arches of the main or altar room, be they the choir arches – are supported by a whole pilaster or a part of it. This principle of construction is pursued by Brunelleschi with such consistency that the width of the arches is evident in the number of flutes: one flute corresponds to each of the small wall arches in the altar room, three correspond to the semi-circular wall arches and six flutes correspond to the choir arch. Such consistency in the connection between the arches and the wall is quite unusual. It was not known either in the classical period or in early Christian or Florentine Romanesque art. On the contrary, Brunelleschi used as his model the Gothic respond-rib system which he found ready-formulated in

exemplary fashion in Florence Cathedral. But instead of responds, the quarter, half or three-quarter pillars which are assigned to a load-bearing element – a column for example – and which continue in the ribs of the dome, Brunelleschi used Corinthian fluted pilasters which are unknown in Gothic, but used in classical architecture. Here it becomes more than evident that Renaissance architecture should not be understood simply as a return to the classical age in reaction to the Gothic. Brunelleschi in particular combines what is considered to be incompatible, the classical with the Gothic language of form. The wall opposite the choir remains free of pilasters (ill. 57). Three consoles which support the architrave here replace the pilasters which mark the entrance to the choir space.

The contrapostal elements of the vertical and horizontal lines are supplemented by the third geometrical form of the circle. The pendentives in the main chamber contain Donatello's medallions, those in the choir room the shells (ill. 60). They circle the domes as it were.

The many small oculi between the ribs of the main dome also belong to it and it is concluded by the lantern (ill. 59).

The basic geometrical forms of circle, vertical lines and horizontal lines, cube and hemisphere are linked according to strict rules and in a balanced relationship to produce complete harmony, avoiding any rigidity. On the contrary, it produces a clarity which liberates the spirit. In this context the coat of arms of the Medici – below the tondi – stands out in particular. It is foreign to the canon of forms, and yet part of it. When Giotto painted the frescoes of the Arena chapel in Padua he gave the donor, Enrico Scrovegni, a place within the program of paintings. He appears below the Last Judgment in the stance of *Humilitas*, humility. A coat of arms in any position within this cycle of frescoes would be unimaginable, but not so in the *Old Sacristy* of Giovanni di Bicci de' Medici: two examples from two centuries which give proof of the changing view of the importance of the individual.

57 (opposite) *Old Sacristy*, view into the main chamber to the wall opposite the apse

There was originally no provision for interior decoration of this building consisting of basic geometrical forms (cube and circle), classical building elements (pilaster and entablature) and the definite link between vault and wall. Brunelleschi here presents his own concept of walls by making a clear distinction between the architectural sections and the empty wall area. The former are made of *pietra serena*, blue-gray sandstone, the latter are given a light whitewash. The plaster hardly allows the material character of the wall to emerge. The wall area with its pilasters, architrave and consoles recalls, rather, a framed empty picture.

58 (below) *Old Sacristy*
Ground plan (according to Geymüller)

The basic shape of the main chamber is a square whose side measures 20 Florentine cubits (11.68 m). Brunelleschi's *Old Sacristy* – so called after Michelangelo had built the *"New" Sacristy* – caused astonishment even as it was being built. Manetti reports: "Due to its new form and its beauty it caused wonder among everyone, citizen or stranger, and a constant stream of people came which caused a great nuisance to those who were working on it."

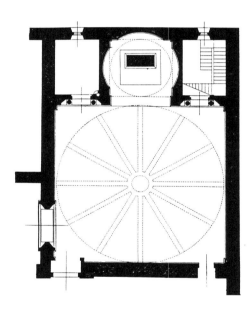

59 (right) *Old Sacristy*, view of the dome of the main chamber

If Brunelleschi had had his way, the tondi in the pendentive zone would have remained empty. Their circular form was intended merely to prepare for the circle of the dome which has its apex in the circle under the lantern. The twelve oculi, which are positioned in the individual sections of the umbrella dome, encircle the center. They also provide light for the *Old Sacristy* together with the dome oculus.

The *Old Sacristy* is – as are almost all buildings by Filippo Brunelleschi – built of gray sandstone. Its plastered walls were intended to act as bare, white surfaces. This is based on the architectural program of Brunelleschi the purist, for it applies also to the domes and not only to the walls. An exception is the one in the choir room (ill. 60), which does not however display the traditional iconography. Its painting shows an exact constellation of the stars on the day when the foundation stone was laid on 9 July 1422, together with the classical gods and demigods of the firmament. The light, possibly white surface has its own fundamental value; it is not there as a "surface to be filled" (Klotz), as was still the case in the 14th century, but it allows the architectural elements – pilasters, architraves or arches – to achieve their full effect. The architecture speaks for itself if the observer is only willing to listen. In this respect the architect and master builder Brunelleschi left painters or sculptors no room for later additions. He did not envisage architecture as the stage for painting to display itself. It is known, for instance, that Brunelleschi disapproved of the sculptural work which his friend Donatello later carried out for the *Old Sacristy* (ill. 56). Some role may have been played in this by the failure to include him as the architect when the furnishing of the rooms which he had built was discussed. But that was not the decisive factor. For he – rightly – held the view that the two doors with the Ionic columns and the massive tympanon, which lead to the side chambers, appear too heavy with the reliefs inserted above them. It is surprising that Brunelleschi does not voice further criticism. The Ionic columns and the triangular pediments cannot be integrated into a consistently executed composition; they spoil the effect like a foreign body.

60 (opposite) *Old Sacristy*, view of the domes in the two chambers

The two vaulted areas are different but have a lot in common. The large circle of the light dome, divided by ribs, with its oculi and the lantern oculus, corresponds to the small circle in the altar room which is filled by a dark fresco depicting the constellation of the night sky over Florence on 9 July 1422. The conch pictures appear in the small chamber in analogy to the tondi.

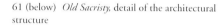

61 (below) *Old Sacristy*, detail of the architectural structure

Remains of the original roofing over the dome of the apse, seen from the present loft.

62 (right) *Old Sacristy*, view from the transept roof of San Lorenzo to the main dome with the lantern, dated 1428 on the architrave

The lantern of the *Old Sacristy*, which was restored from 1939 to 1940, follows the classical Florentine model of the Baptistery lantern, as does the one on the *Pazzi Chapel* (ill. 71). Both are designed as "circular aedicules". In view of these two traditional examples, what Brunelleschi is able to make of the design of the lantern on the cathedral is all the more remarkable.

The extent to which Brunelleschi is ahead of Renaissance thinking is clearly evident in particular in the importance which he ascribes to the color white. Around 1450, Leon Battista Alberti, to whom we owe the most important treatise on painting of that time, also wrote a treatise on architecture. Quoting Cicero, who in turn quotes Plato, he describes white as the proper color for a temple – his synonym for church – and continues "that the divinities find greatest pleasure in the purity and simplicity of color and of life equally". Alberti believes that he must "remind his followers through rules that they should throw away idle ornamentation and trumpery and should make room above all for the lustre of simple white." By giving a new significance to the white wall, by making it an important effect in his system of elevation, Brunelleschi turns it into an object of artistic reflection, of architectural theory. Against this background it is no surprise that Brunelleschi sets out in writing that the portico vault in his first building – the *Ospedale degli Innocenti* – should be white.

63 Luca della Robbia
Madonna of the Apple, ca. 1460
Terracotta, glazed, 70 x 52 cm
Museo Nazionale del Bargello, Florence

This depiction of the Madonna became part of the Medici collection even before the end of the sixteenth century. The relief was sculpted in one piece, the white figures and the blue background produced together. The eyes of the Madonna and the Christ child are emphasized in gray-blue and purple. In Christian iconography the apple in the hand of Jesus represents a reference to the overcoming of and redemption from sin. The Christ child presses it firmly with both hands against his mother's breast and looks expectantly upwards to the right.

Luca della Robbia was among the most famous sculptors of his time. He was born in Florence in 1399 or 1400 and came from a wool merchant's family of the bourgeoisie. Little is known about his artistic training. He probably worked as an apprentice in the workshop of Lorenzo Ghiberti and Nanni di Banco (ca. 1375–1421), whose work had a lasting effect on him. In the mid-fifteenth century these were the two most renowned workshops where an apprentice could learn how to handle bronze and marble.

When della Robbia was commissioned to undertake the singer's gallery for Florence cathedral in 1431, he was already a recognized artist, according to the sources. The so-called *Cantoria* is his earliest surviving work. But aside from his marble and bronze works, such as the north door of the sacristy of Florence cathedral (1446–1449), it was above all his glazed terracotta which made della Robbia famous. He experimented with this technique for the first time in the 1430s and gradually brought it to perfection.

Terracotta, fired clay, was traditionally closely connected with bronze casting. Smaller clay models were part of the sculptural work process and preceded the finished statue. The clay model was covered all over by a layer of wax into which the artist sculpted all the details. This layer of wax was covered in several coatings of fine clay so that a single casting mold was created. If the whole thing was heated, the wax flowed out and the artist poured the molten bronze into the space which had thus been created between the mold and the core.

Della Robbia gradually removed the clay model from this process and thus created an independent genre. As clay was cheap, the use of these terracottas as new sculptures in their own right quickly spread. Colored ceramics inspired della Robbia to glaze his sculptures, mostly in white, blue and green. But he kept the way in which they were produced as a secret of his workshop.

Half-length depictions of the Madonna were very popular in fifteenth century Florence. The number of those which have been preserved alone makes the conclusion very likely that there was hardly a well-off house or oratory (chapel for private prayer) at that time which did not possess such a marble, stucco or terracotta relief. They began to be produced commercially after 1420: the reliefs were sculpted in the sculptors' workshops and subsequently colored by painters. Della Robbia's reliefs of the Madonna – executed as terracottas from the 1440s onwards (ills. 63, 64) – are among his strongest and most well-known works. Over a period of almost fifty years they were created for a market which was dominated by Ghiberti and Donatello, but which other artists such as Desiderio da Settignano (1428/31–1464) Antonio Rossellino (1427–1479) and others were also jostling to enter. We must, however, distinguish between single pieces

and those which were intended for reproduction. Remarkably, della Robbia worked together with Buggiano in the 1430s, so that a number of reliefs were created which are in turn ascribed to Brunelleschi's adopted son and Luca della Robbia.

His nephew Andrea (1435–1525) began to work with him during his lifetime. Almost 30 years after Brunelleschi's death and the completion of the *Ospedale degli Innocenti,* the tondi, which had been empty until then, were decorated, although we do not know for certain whether this was Brunelleschi's intention.

Andrea della Robbia was recommended by numerous similar commissions (ill. 67). He continued the family tradition after Luca's death (1482), as did the eldest son Giovanni (1469–after 1525), who helped to popularize the glazed terracottas. As well as the pieces produced by the workshop itself, the use of models as a recognizable trade mark was a key element.

The first documented terracotta by Luca della Robbia is *The Resurrection of Christ* (ill. 65). This relief was created between 1442 and 1445 for the lunette above the entrance to the northern sacristy of Florence cathedral. At 200 x 260 cm it is of considerable size. The greater than life-size figures have been executed in white on a blue background. With its economy and few colors, details such as the highlights in the eyes, on the wings of the angels and in the aureole around Christ are emphasized. Luca's intention – which was also the reason for his immediate success – was to compete at a much lower price with the marble sculptures which were given similar coloring at that time, particularly in the interior.

It is unlikely that Luca would have been commissioned to undertake *The Resurrection of Christ* if previous works had not provided evidence of his skill in this medium.

The tondi of the apostles in Brunelleschi's Pazzi Chapel represent a group of reliefs, some of which were created at an earlier time. The glazed terracotta figures depict two clear groups. The first one comprises the twelve apostles on the walls, which are probably part of Brunelleschi's own ideas of how the interior ought to be designed. The second group comprises the four Evangelists in the pendentives, the terracotta decoration in the small dome of a portico and the tondo of St. Andrew above the entrance to the chapel. Architect and sculptor were in agreement about the relationship between the architecture and the sculptural decoration. The tondi were not intended to disturb the architectural balance but to emphasize it in a harmonious way. Thus the colors are restricted to white and blue and the figures, all in frontal view, sit on horizontal strips of cloud.

On entering the Pazzi Chapel, *St. Matthew* (ill. 66) and St. Peter can be seen to the left of the altar and John the

64 Andrea della Robbia
Madonna of the Stonemasons, 1475–1480
Terracotta, glazed, 134 x 96 cm
Museo Nazionale del Bargello, Florence

The Madonna with the Christ child was commissioned by the guild of stonemasons. The emblems in the tondi refer to the associated professions of architect, stonemason, sculptor and mason. The Madonna sits in a semi-niche, flanked by puttos. Intimately connected to the Christ child and with her sorrowful expression indicating the Passion which lies ahead, she embodies the *Mater Eleusea* type of Madonna, the compassionate Madonna. Above the grouped figures, the hands of God the Father and the dove of the Holy Spirit appear in the heaven zone.
The flower decoration surrounding the sculpture rises from two vases at the bottom of the frame and is symbolically connected to Christ and Mary with its entwining roses.

Evangelist and James the Elder on the right. St. Andrew and James the Younger are depicted on the right wall, the apostles Simon, Thaddeus, Thomas and Philip from left to right on the entrance side, and St. Matthias and St. Bartholomew on the left wall. Few interior spaces of the early Renaissance have such clarity and cheerfulness as the Pazzi Chapel. While this must be ascribed to Brunelleschi's creative power, Luca della Robbia must be given credit for the solemn mood. His art made the co-existence of architecture and sculpture succeed.

65 Luca della Robbia
The Resurrection of Christ, 1442–1445
Terracotta, glazed, 200 x 265 cm
Santa Maria del Fiore, Florence

The scene is inscribed in the lunette. Christ the Triumphant – blessing with his right hand, carrying the banner with the cross in his left – is the focus of the picture. He is symmetrically flanked by angels. The composition of the remaining scene in a semi-circle follows the shape of the lunette on the one hand, and emphasizes the central figure of Christ on the other. The figures, glazed in white, provide an effective contrast to the blue background. The three-dimensional effect of the elements in relief, such as the clouds at the feet of Christ and the angels, is emphasized by the use of a

lighter blue. The original gilding of the surface, lost today, was used to represent details such as the naturalistic depiction of the aureole around Christ or the highlights on the wings of the angels. Luca's *Resurrection* is one of the most significant depictions of this important subject in Christian iconography and accordingly also assumed a model function. Both Andrea del Castagno's *Resurrection* in Sant'Apollonia (1445–1459) and Piero della Francesca's in Borgo San Sepolero (ca. 1460) can be traced back to this lunette relief.

66 Luca della Robbia
St. Matthew, after 1445
Terracotta, glazed, diameter: 134 cm
Santa Croce, Cappella Pazzi, Florence

The tondo of *St. Matthew* is among the most beautiful in
the Pazzi Chapel. The seated saint appears white against a
blue background, his head lowered and turned to the side.
The quill in his right hand and the open book in his left
show him to be the Evangelist. Thoughtfully he looks at
what he has written. An angel kneels to his left on a cloud
which serves him as a seat. The angel is the symbol of
Matthew. The angel holds an inkpot in one hand and
points to the hands of the saint with the other. In this way
the divine messenger indicates that the Evangelist is
writing about the Son of God – about the life, work and
death of Jesus Christ.

67 Andrea della Robbia
Infant, 1487
Terracotta, glazed, diameter: 146 cm
Ospedale degli Innocenti, Piazza SS. Annunziata,
Florence

The medallions with the foundlings are positioned in the
spandrels on the front of the foundling hospital. Like all
the others, this upright boy stands out in almost full relief
from the background in neutral blue. He is wrapped in
swaddling clothes from his feet to his middle. His arms
are stretched out and he has turned his slightly inclined
head to the side. His gaze has no definite focus. All of this
gives him an expression of helplessness. By making them
artistically different, Andrea della Robbia prevents the
impression of monotony in his depiction of the infants.
In this way they supplement the façade of the foundling
hospital as sculptural decoration.

THE PAZZI CHAPEL

68 (left) *Pazzi Chapel*, planned ca. 1429, construction started ca. 1442
Santa Croce, first cloister, Florence

The chapel, the bell tower and the monastery courtyard of Santa Croce: the arch of the chapel porch cross refers to the arches of the cloister so that the porch, surprising in a monastery courtyard, can be considered part of the cloister.

Just as Brunelleschi's two basilicas of *San Lorenzo* and *Santo Spirito* (ills. 33, 40) are related, so the *Old Sacristy* and the *Pazzi Chapel* are also linked. Around 1429 Andrea Pazzi commissioned Brunelleschi to build a chapter house in the monastery courtyard of Santa Croce. Such a building was originally used for instructing the monks or to read from the rules of the order. But this commission extended the function of the space, which then no longer served merely as a meeting place but also for private devotion. The entrance to the small room of the Pazzi lies to the right of the altar (ill. 72). At the same time the reference to its use as chapter house cannot be ignored. In the main room the pilasters rest on a stone bench which goes along all the walls with the exception of the entrance area opposite the altar room (ill. 74). The inspiration for Brunelleschi's creative achievement was, interestingly, a medieval model, the Dominican monastery Santa Maria Novella in Florence, built between 1348 and 1355. The chapter house was paid for by Buonamico di Lapo Guidalotti; however, as it was put at the disposal of Eleonora of Toledo, wife of Cosimo de' Medici, and her entourage, it has since been known as the "Spanish Chapel".

While the construction of the *Old Sacristy* was concluded in ten years, it took as long with the *Pazzi Chapel* for building even to start (about 1442). It is uncertain whether the interior was indeed finished by 1444. Work appears to have been finally concluded around 1469, more than two decades after Brunelleschi's death. The *Pazzi Chapel* is thus not a pure work by Brunelleschi. As so often, his successors completed what he had started. Brunelleschi was succeeded by Michelozzo (1396–1472) who took his place as architect and master builder after his death. He, in turn, was succeeded by Giuliano da Maciano. The restoration of the *Pazzi Chapel* in the 19th century finished it off. Some parts of the building have dates which mean that they cannot be ascribed to Brunelleschi. Thus the drum of the dome bears the date 1459 and on the vault in the porch the figure 1461 has been carved. Yet it is precisely the façade of this portico (ill. 70) which has become the best-known element of the chapel. It is very easy to go into raptures over it:

69 (opposite) *Pazzi Chapel*, external view

The exterior of the chapel as it is today, the result of the extensive building work which was not finished until ca. 1470, of the changes made in earlier periods and of restoration in the 19th century.

70 (opposite) *Pazzi Chapel*, porch

Six delicate pillars carry an entablature which is followed by an attic broken by an arch. This hides a panelled barrel vault based on the Roman model which is interrupted in the center by a dome decorated with majolica rosettes. The inscribed date on the dome shows that the portico was erected as late as 1461, probably by the workshop of Bernardo Rosselino (1409–1464), which was engaged on other work for Santa Croce as well.

71 (right) *Pazzi Chapel*, view from the campanile of Santa Croce to the dome roof with lantern

"Brunelleschi used pillars and pilasters and arches to create a new whole which is of a lightness and gracefulness which separates this building from everything that went before." (Gombrich). The pilasters, which rise up between upright rectangular rounded windows, project from the wall and relate to the pillars at the front; the open space between them finds its counterpart in the window openings of the wall. An architrave rests on the pillars, equivalent to the cornice on the wall of the building at the back. It is broken in the middle by an archivolt, a decorated arch. This clearly extends higher than the framed entry door which is finished off by a triangular pediment. The attic is structured by a blind order and small, Corinthian double pilasters, whose number corresponds to the pillars below. It is finished off by a richly ornamented entablature.

The portico with its triumphal arch motif had considerable impact. Alberti provided variations of this form of façade in his buildings, for example in the Tempio Malatestino, as it is known, near San Francesco in Rimini, begun in 1450. Brunelleschi may have planned it, but he would probably have executed it differently. The complete entablature over the small pilasters of the attic is unusual in his buildings. If we recall the façade of the *Ospedale degli Innocenti*, we would rather expect to see a molded cornice in its place. This would also make the proportions more

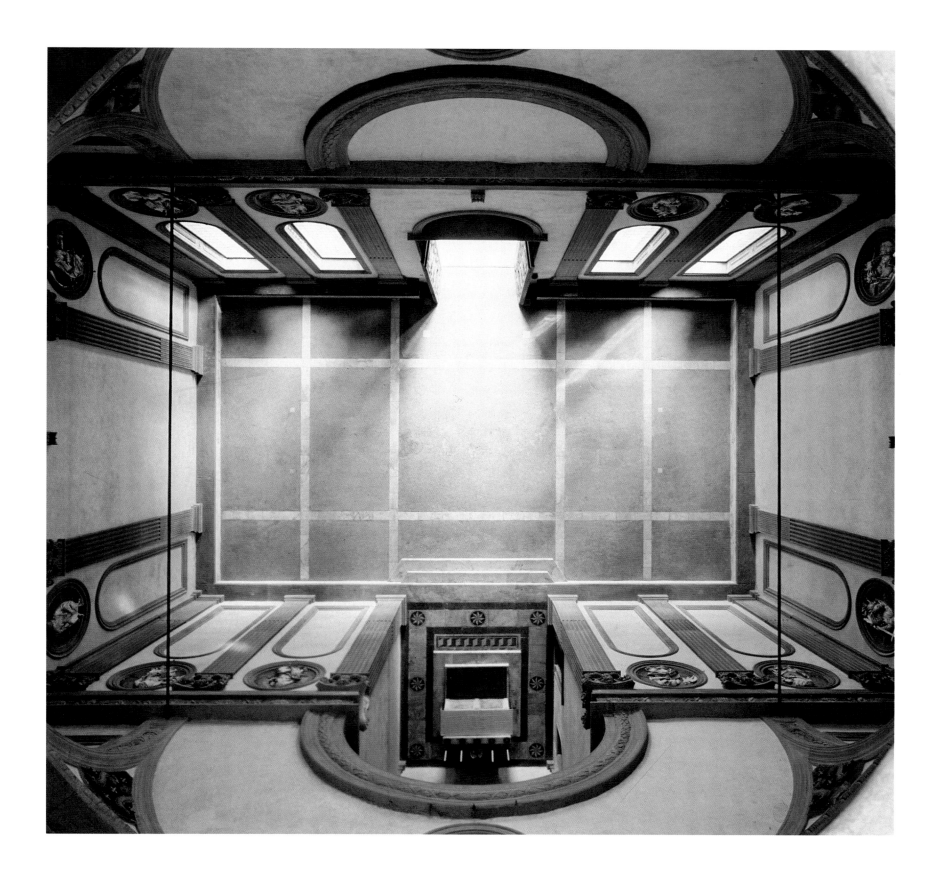

72 (opposite) *Pazzi Chapel*, view of the main chamber and choir room

As in the *Old Sacristy*, the entablature of the main chamber continues in the choir chapel. It was a remarkable idea of Brunelleschi's to choose the stone benches used for seating by the fathers as a plinth for the pilasters. Since the height of the benches corresponds to the height of the steps leading to the choir room, the pilasters of both rooms start at the same level, which gives them identical proportions.

73 (above) *Pazzi Chapel*, view from above into the two chambers

The *Pazzi Chapel* has a clear structure down to details such as the floor patterns. We can for instance read off from the floor the position of the pilasters on the walls and the size of the areas which they subdivide. This demonstrates the regular geometrical patterns and simple relationships of proportion from which the space is created. The light which enters sets the architecture in motion so that the bright reflecting walls appear to shine by themselves in contrast to the elements of the building – for instance the pilasters.

harmonious. The panelling of the vaulting is unusual in Brunelleschi's architectural language. It is, moreover, too heavy for the six Corinthian pillars, one of which had to be replaced for this reason. Would we expect something like this from an architect who knew how to vault the dome of Florence Cathedral?

There are remarkable correspondences and differences between the ground plan and elevation of the *Old Sacristy* and the *Pazzi Chapel* (ills. 58, 72). Inside, Brunelleschi continued to develop formal principles which he had begun to formulate in the Medici Chapel. Thus the main chamber has arcades not only on the choir wall but on all four sides. It is, however, no longer a square – as before – but a rectangle. This changes the proportions and they lack the compelling logic of the large chamber in the *Old Sacristy*. Although the middle

bay of the *Pazzi Chapel* is vaulted by a dome, it is not an umbrella dome as before but a pendentive dome. It rises to such an extent that it blocks the lower part of a window which has thus been bricked off today. If the dome had another shape, the window would be uncovered. For this reason the literature suggests that a suspended dome might have been planned instead of a pendentive one. Its vertex would be clearly lower as the suspended spandrels are not an independent part of the construction. And since the dome does not cover the whole space, the barrel vaults which flank it to the left and right become necessary.

The *Pazzi Chapel* thus shows weaknesses in its composition when compared to the *Old Sacristy*. These inconsistencies illustrate the fact that it lacks the harmonious cohesion which characterizes the *Old Sacristy*.

74 (above) *Pazzi Chapel*, view of the choir wall

The frieze, the horizontal, ornamented strip of the entablature, shows the lamb of Christ on the altar with seven seals and seraphim, six-winged visionary beings which surround the throne of God. The walls thus present a remarkable iconographic program. The twelve apostles appear under the lamb of God, and below them the fathers sit on the stone benches. A clear hierarchical structure is evident, illustrating the larger context in which the place was to serve as monastery meeting room.

75 (opposite) *Pazzi Chapel*, view of the main chamber: structure of wall

Not only does the motif of the arches appear above the choir entrance in the *Pazzi Chapel*, it also belongs to the other three walls. It is repeated there in the form of blind arches. The vaulting of the barrel vault also takes up the semi-circle produced by the pendentives. The windows are architecturally framed, their frames recur in the blind windows. Open and closed wall areas provide a regular structure to the space.

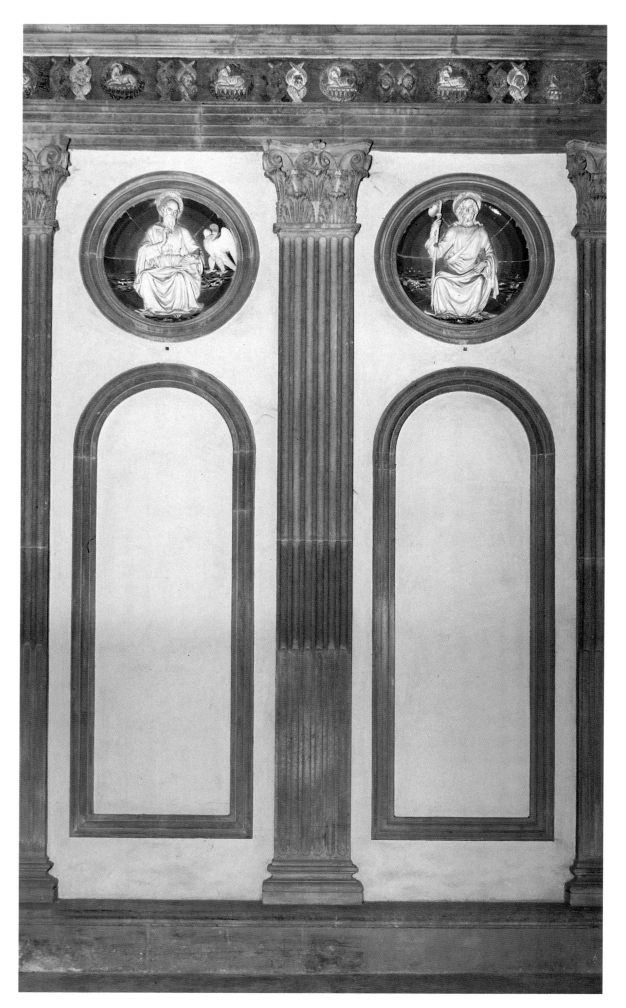

76 (left) *Pazzi Chapel,* view of the long wall opposite the entrance with the choir entrance

The terracotta tondi, which are distributed over all four walls of the main chamber – four on each long side, two on each transverse wall – show the twelve apostles. The tondi, executed by Luca della Robbia (1399/1400–1482) fit in well with the architecture since they vary and strengthen its dual harmony of color, the blue-gray sandstone and light whitewash, into a stronger blue-white.

77 (opposite) *Pazzi Chapel,* view of the domes

The medallions of the pendentives in the main chamber show the four evangelists. These were produced by the workshop of della Robbia, but Brunelleschi may have created the models for them himself. Whereas the oculi in the *Old Sacristy* are covered by open-work iron plates (ill. 60) with the task of filtering the incoming light, the round windows in the large dome of the *Pazzi Chapel* are uncovered. Thus a large part of the light, which makes a key contribution to the overall impression of the space, here falls from above.

SANTA MARIA DEGLI ANGELI

78 Santa Maria degli Angeli
External view, Codice Rustichi, ca. 1450
Biblioteca del Seminario maggiore, Florence

The Florentine merchant Marco di Barolomeo Rustichi compiled the codex named after him, which can be regarded as an illustrated city guide of Florence. Originally Santa Maria degli Angeli was to have been built separately in a place to the west of the monastery. According to a document dated 15 May 1434 this site was rejected. Thus Brunelleschi's polygon found its place in the wall which surrounds the monastery buildings – as in the illustration.

Brunelleschi began the construction of *Santa Maria degli Angeli* in 1434, but three years later the work had to be stopped. Funding was no longer guaranteed. It was to have come from the legacy of the Florentine merchants Matteo and Andrea Scolari, but the sum which they had donated for the building was confiscated in 1437 because it was required for the war against Lucca. Building work was never resumed and the torso of the building, completed to a height of seven meters, became the "strangest creation of the early Renaissance" (Heydenreich).

Brunelleschi allegedly left the drawings and the model for his project to the monks of the neighboring monastery. Since neither has been preserved, we must refer to other sources in order to get some idea of what Brunelleschi intended to realize with this late work of his.

The Codex Rustichi dates from about 1450 (ill. 82). It contains an external view of *Santa Maria degli Angeli* which is, however, very summary and some of whose details lead to the conclusion that we are dealing with an early but inexact attempt at the reconstruction of the unfinished building. Of greater help is a ground plan and elevation which we owe to Giuliano da Sangallo (ill. 80).

Brunelleschi designed *Santa Maria degli Angeli* as a centralized building, thus creating the earliest design in the architecture of the early Renaissance of a building with a completely centralized composition: an octagon around which eight square chapels are placed. High pilaster arcades open them to the octagonal chamber. The floor area of the chapels affects the whole building. It expands the external view of the eight-sided building into one with sixteen sides and it creates gaps which divide the chapels from one another. These gaps are formed into three semi-circular niches, two of them connected to the chapels, the third one inserted in the external wall. The former are connected by a passageway which thus becomes a gallery around the center. The ground plan and the ground floor walls of *Santa Maria degli Angeli* were sufficient to fascinate generations of later architects. The effect was so profound that we know of drawings by Leonardo for churches with an octagonal structure (ill. 83).

In the literature, we find two different approaches to an assessment of the polygon. This building project by Brunelleschi is seen either as a continuation of medieval works or as a revival of classical architecture. The second assumption is the more common one. It is very closely linked to the question: When did Brunelleschi encounter Roman classicism, and what are the dates of the Roman journeys?

According to Manetti, and Vasari, who follows him, the artist spent time in the Eternal City at a very early stage and continued to visit the city for study purposes. He is said to have left for Rome the first time after he lost the competition for the Baptistery door. But there are doubts about such a journey in 1401 or 1402, not only because there is no evidence for them. There are too many reasons why he should not have gone, including above all the character of his early works and the conditions in the city at the time of the schism. During the last two decades of the schism, the split into the Greek Orthodox and Roman Catholic churches (1378–1417), fewer than 15,000 people lived in the Eternal City. They were completely impoverished and even the clergy lacked the barest of necessities. The Roman streets were therefore anything but safe.

The connections which Manetti draws in his description look very much like artistic license: the initial rejection of his art by his native city; the subsequent withdrawal which at the same time takes the form of a departure to a new city in order to study classical art, recognized as a model, there; the concern from a distance with the question how the cathedral dome is to be vaulted.

And there is something else which must be taken into account. An early study of past greatness is an essential condition for anyone representing the renewal of architecture in the classical spirit, which Brunelleschi undoubtedly did for Manetti. But this does not necessarily correspond with Brunelleschi's actual development as an architect. For we have evidence that he visited Rome in the years immediately preceding the work on *Santa Maria degli Angeli*, the period from 1432 to 1434. In accordance with this, the impressions which he gained at that time could have been expressed immediately in the building design. If *Santa Maria degli*

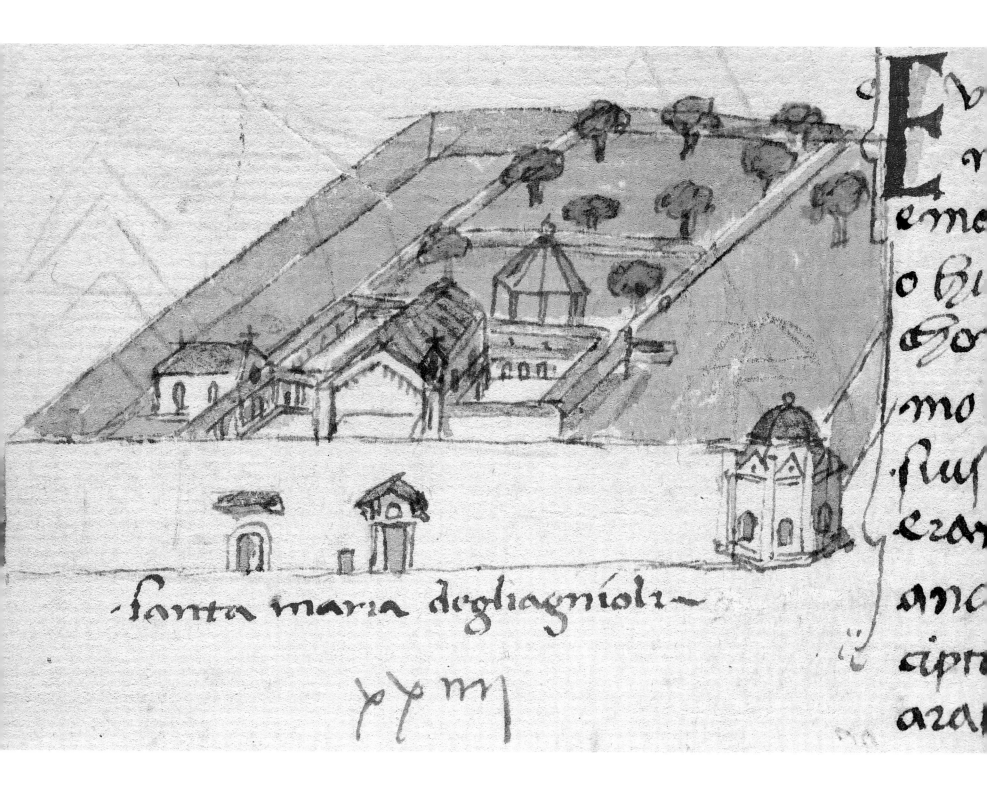

santa maria degliagnioli

xxviij

79 *Santa Maria degli Angeli*, interior view: a niche with the passage between the side chapels

The interior design of *Santa Maria degli Angeli* was supplemented and renewed at the end of the 1430s. But the architrave of the door is still the original; the powerful moldings of the door frame and plinth correspond to the massive nature of the building.

82 (right) *Santa Maria degli Angeli* (cf. ill. 78)
External view, Codice Rustichi, ca. 1450
Biblioteca del Seminario maggiore, Florence

If the façade shown here is related to the ground plan, the question arises how the two can be reconciled. Do the triangular pediments and the delicate small towers which arise between them fit with the massive building which was planned for *Santa Maria degli Angeli*?

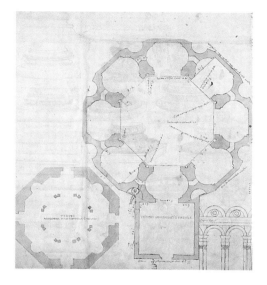

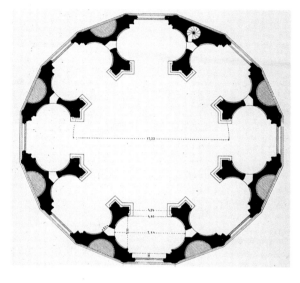

80 (above left) Giuliano da Sangallo
Ground plan and elevation of *Santa Maria degli Angeli* and ground plan of the Baptistery of Bologna, 1492–94
Codice Vaticano Latino Barberiniano 4424, fol. 15 v
Biblioteca Apostolica Vaticana, Rome

Da Sangallo's sheet gives an impression of the possible internal structure of the church. The elevation shows two sides of the octagon. The most noticeable features are the blind arches which reach from their supports beyond the entablature and are taken around the round windows.

81 (above, center) *Santa Maria degli Angeli*, ground plan, construction started 1434, ceased 1437
Via degli Alfani, corner of Via del Castellacio, Florence

In *Santa Maria degli Angeli* Brunelleschi created the earliest example in Renaissance architecture of a purely centralized building: an octagon surrounded by eight chapels. These have side entrances which link the chapels to each other and are expanded by the niches built into the wall. This method of giving sculptural life to the wall by means of concave and convex forms characterizes the building as one of Brunelleschi's late works.

Angeli had been finished, it would have been a building of unmistakable Roman characteristics, with proportions which would have presented a deliberate weightiness. The slim, delicate pillars from earlier buildings have given way to pilasters which are set in front of the massive columns in the corners of the octagonal space. Such columns have classical models, such as for instance the Pantheon (AD 118–128) in Rome. By resuming construction of classical columns, Filippo Brunelleschi bids a decisive farewell to Gothic architecture. This can be seen in the construction of the church. For the first time in Brunelleschi's work we encounter double pilasters (ill. 79) instead of the usual folded simple ones – compare the large chamber of the *Old Sacristy* with that of *Santa Maria degli Angeli*. The door frames, plinth and entablature show strong moldings (ill. 79), and the dome was planned as a heavy shell. In accordance with the domes of the Pantheon or of the so-called temple of Minerva Medica (ca. AD 320), it was to be built with solid walls. The extent of the contrast with the Gothic style can be seen immediately if we think of the dome of Florence Cathedral, which Brunelleschi vaulted with two shells, an inner and an outer one.

That *Santa Maria degli Angeli* is conceived of "wholly in terms of mass" (Heydenreich) is nowhere as clear as in the chapels which almost represent incisions in the external wall. Brunelleschi is here working *with* the wall; it is not boundary and conclusion of a space but has itself become something which forms space within the overall spatial composition.

Two classical buildings, the Pantheon and the Minerva Medica, may be possible models. We do not know of a direct model to which Brunelleschi's bold design could be related. It must also be born in mind that there were many more Roman ruins in his time than we know of today. He may have received his impressions from works of which we are no longer aware. It should also be taken into consideration that it was a long time after Brunelleschi's death before classical works were thought of in terms of monuments – irrespective of the common view that the reception of the classical period provided one of the stimuli for Renaissance art. The famous Laocoon group, for instance, was found as early as 1496 but only recovered ten years later. And it is not until 1512 that Raphael is appointed by papal letter as superintendent of all classical works found in papal domains.

83 Leonardo da Vinci
Centralized building design for a church with central
octagon and eight chapels, ca. 1490 or later
Ms. B. fol. 17v. (Paris Manuscript B)
Institut de France, Paris

In Florence, Leonardo (1452–1519) studied the
Brunelleschi churches of *Santo Spirito* and *Santa Maria
degli Angeli*, drawing their ground plans, and in Milan he
investigated Filarete's (ca. 1400–1469) projects. The
results of these studies may be seen in the inventive
architectural designs in his sketch books, none of which –
as far as we know – were ever carried out. They show
various plans for centralized buildings, including this
design of a church with a central octagon and eight
surrounding chapels.

The centralized building, the church which develops
uniformly in all directions from a vertical central axis, was
the ideal of Renaissance architects. This is verified by the
fact that Leon Battista Alberti constantly refers to round and
polygonal buildings in his treatise "De re aedificatoria"
(published in ca. 1450, 1485), "On architecture", which
contains the "first complete program of the Renaissance
church" (Wittkower). The architectural theoretician was
not alone in this. His ideas were put into practice, as is
shown by many buildings. The *Tempietto of St. Peter's*
(1502) by Bramante (1485–1514) and *San Biagio* near
Montepulciano (1518–45) by Antonio di Sangallo the elder
(1485–1546) are two impressive examples.

Based on a centralized composition, a building could be
realized in the purest form and with absolute symmetry
using stereometric elements – such as cubes, cylinders or
hemispheres. And symmetry was one of the main concerns
of the Renaissance, a central requirement of its ideal of
beauty.

Yet the centralized building is not an invention of the 15th
century. This genre – as well as the basilica which also retains
its importance in the Renaissance – had been in use since
the early Christian classical period, even if relatively rarely.
It is only with the advent of Gothic architecture that it
disappears almost completely.

The ground plan of a church, a medieval basilica for
instance, reveals much about the tasks for which it was
intended. One of them was to guide the faithful to the altar,
which is most often positioned in the east, while the former
enter the space of the church from the west. Centralized
composition negates this spatial tendency; indeed, there is
fundamentally no movement in any specific direction: "The
space only achieves its full effect if it is observed from the
center." (Pevsner). The result is that the transcendental
meaning of the church – as displayed for instance in an apse
mosaic – has made way for an immanent one. In a
centralized building of the Renaissance, human beings
perceive themselves at the center of surrounding beauty
which is well proportioned, meaning that it is composed
according to human measure. If they immerse themselves

in it by looking, they experience the extent to which human
beings have become the measure of all things. This claim
also underlies the literature of the time: Machiavelli's "Il
principe" ("The Prince"), written in 1513 and published in
1532, draws the image of the ideal prince, the perfect ruler.
And Baldassare Castiglione describes the perfect courtier in
his "Il libro del cortegiano" ("The book of the courtier"),
written between 1508 and 1516, and published in a revised
version in 1528. In this context it is no surprise that *the*
church of the Christian west, St. Peter's in Rome, was at
various planning stages in the 16th century going to be
built as a centralized building. Bramante's ideas (1506)
introduced a centralized composition (ill. 84) right from the
start in the form of a block building following the ancient
Roman model – the first instance in the high Renaissance
and just as Brunelleschi had demonstrated it in *Santa Maria
degli Angeli* (ill. 81). After his death, Raphael (1483–1528)
rejected these plans. He was thinking of a basilica with
a centralized choir. His successor, Baldassare Peruzzi
(1481–1536), took up the scheme for a centralized building
again, which was followed by a further basilica project with
the wooden model by Antonio da Sangallo the elder. The
idea of the centralized building returns (ill. 85) – though
transformed – with Michelangelo (1475–1564), who was
architect and master builder from 1547 onwards. Not until
the intervention of Carlo Maderna (1556–1629) does
the basilica plan finally win in the early 17th century: "A
centralized building had been and remained close above all
to the heart of the community of artists. But the papacy had
more to represent, namely the totality of the faithful. For
them, however, the basilica was the long-revered symbol of
their belief." (Paatz).

Yet Brunelleschi's late work, *Santa Maria degli Angeli*,
nevertheless introduces the triumphant progress of the
centralized building. The age of humanism, that movement
which – guided by the classical period – arises in the mid-
14th century and lasts until the 17th century, taking as its
model human beings and their purpose, primarily in this
world rather than the next, could not have found a more
fitting architectural expression for itself.

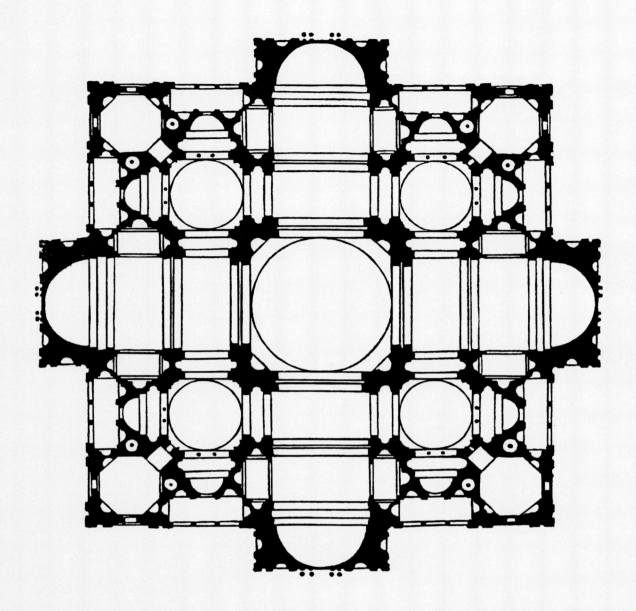

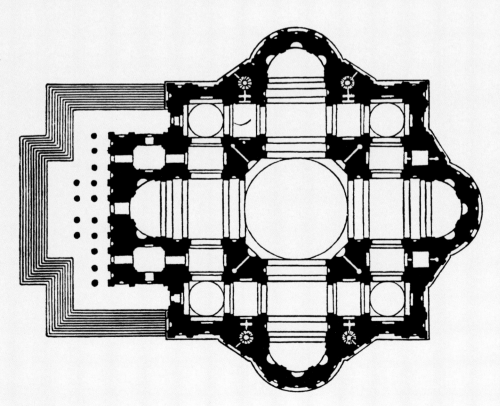

84 (left) Bramante
Ground plan for *San Pietro* in Rome, 1506

Donato d'Angelo Lazzari, known as Bramante (1444–1514), bases his design of Christianity's main church on a Greek cross, the four apses of which are structured with such strict symmetry that it is impossible to see from the ground plan which one of them was to contain the high altar. The central dome is surrounded by smaller ones which rise above the corner chapels. These side chapels are also designed in the form of the Greek cross. Two apses can be seen, the other two are intersected by the arms of the central cross. This creates a square gallery which surrounds the mighty central dome. Four corner towers were to rise at the ends of the diagonal axes. They complete the ground plan, making it into a square.

86 (opposite) Cola da Caprarola and others
Santa Maria della Consolazione, 1508
Todi

The church of *Santa Maria della Consolazione* is a fine example of a centrally planned building on the ground plan of a Greek cross. Four semi-circular apses supplement the central square, above which rises a mighty drum with a dome. Thus this religious building represents a type of architecture which was introduced by Giuliano da Sangallo the Elder (ca. 1453–1534) with his church Madonna della Carceri in Prato (started 1484), and variations of which appeared in San Pietro in Rome. There is an astonishing likeness to some architectural designs by Leonardo da Vinci, created only a short time before.

85 (left) Michelangelo
Ground plan for *San Pietro* in Rome, 1546

Michelangelo Buonarotti (1475–1564), took the arms of the Greek cross from Bramante's design. But where Bramante had planned independent subsidiary centers which repeat the main centers on a smaller scale, Michelangelo suppressed the arms of the smaller Greek crosses. He thereby made the central dome with its square gallery dominate the whole space. Michelangelo wanted to decorate the east façade – the church is not oriented (i. e. does not have its high altar to the east) – with an open porch consisting of ten free-standing pillars which was to have a further portico consisting of four pillars, corresponding to the width of the nave, in front of it. This porch would have completely destroyed the ideal symmetry which had been planned by Bramante.

FLORENCE CATHEDRAL: SANTA MARIA DEL FIORE

87 Dome of *Santa Maria del Fiore,* 1420–1436
Florence

Florence Cathedral with Brunelleschi's crowned dome on the one side and Giotto's campanile on the other. Brunelleschi's biographer Manetti was enthusiastic about the dome. It appeared to him "majestic and wonderfully swelling".

THE DOME

While for almost all of Brunelleschi's buildings it is necessary to discover the elements which were changed by his successors, the situation for Florence Cathedral is completely reversed. We have to know at least the broad outline of the history of its construction in order to be able to assess Brunelleschi's achievements. In 1296 Arnolfo di Cambio (ca. 1240–1302) began the construction, on the site of the old basilica of Santa Reparata, of a new cathedral, which was to become the symbol of the city and fill Florentines with pride. The name alone already indicates the extent to which Florence as a city wished to point the way with this church: *Santa Maria del Fiore* – the epithet is an allusion to Fiorenza, the earlier name of the city. The reference is unambiguous.

After di Cambio's death (1302), building work stopped for almost 50 years. Under Francesco Talenti, documented between 1325 and 1369, it was resumed again and the original design of the choir end was enlarged. Giotto's (1267–1337) campanile had already been built at an earlier time, after 1330. The original idea of a nave and two aisles leading to the large dome space – a combination of basilica and centralized building – and the conches, which are distributed polygonally around the center of the dome, goes back to di Cambio.

In 1367, a commission of master builders and painters, *maestri e dipintori,* including Andrea Orcagna (ca. 1308–1368) and Taddeo Gaddi, documented between 1334 and 1366 and a pupil of Giotto, prepared a model which was to lay down the final shape of the cathedral. All leading master builders, the *operai,* henceforth had to swear to keep exactly to this model. This was later to include Brunelleschi. According to the model, a drum was to be inserted between crossing and dome and detailed instructions were drawn up for the construction of the dome itself. Thus the curvature of the vault was to be calculated by the *quinto-acuto* measure, which meant that the radius of curvature at the base of the dome had to be four-fifths of the diameter of the floor area.

In 1415 the moment had arrived. The drum had been built under Giovanni d'Ambrogio and this demonstrated clearly for the first time the extraordinary nature of what was being attempted with the construction of the dome. The building had grown to a height of 52 meters, the thickness of the walls came to almost four meters, the span between two opposite sides of the octagon measured almost 42 meters, and measured to the base of the lantern the dome would rise to a height of more than 80 meters. Was there a master builder who could erect the dome under these conditions?

In order to find the most suitable builder, the cathedral *operai,* the lodge of the cathedral stonemasons, announced a competition in 1418. Ghiberti took part in it as well as Brunelleschi, but this time he did not win. Brunelleschi was able to achieve a decision in his favor with a brick model on which Donatello (1382/86–1466) and Nanni di Banco (1384–1421) had also worked. The incredible feature of his proposed solution was that he intended to build the dome *senza armadura,* without scaffolding. In order to understand what was so special about this proposal, it is necessary to look at the alternatives. One competitor planned the construction of wooden scaffolding from which the work would be done. Another proposed a similar plan: a stone tower which would later be dismantled again. The commission might have had a number of questions with regard to these proposals: is it possible to make reliable calculations from a stone tower, would such mighty wooden scaffolding not collapse under its own weight? These concerns would have turned to incredulity, however, when presented with Brunelleschi's idea. But he was clearly able to convince the commission. This is all the more surprising as Brunelleschi was not able to show any work which would have provided evidence of his suitability for this project. First plans might have existed for some of his early buildings, but none of them had yet been erected. The cathedral *operai* therefore resorted to a position of safety. Ghiberti, who had acquired his reputation as an artist from the time of the Baptistery competition in 1401, was appointed alongside Brunelleschi as equal cathedral architect and master builder.

Opinion is divided as to whether Ghiberti

(1378 – 1455) had any part in the construction of the
cathedral dome. Ghiberti lists his works in the
Commentarii, his autobiography written towards the
end of his life – which is incidentally the first by an artist
in the modern era – and speaks of his work on the dome
as the last item. There are, however, clear indications
that if there was cooperation, it was not very productive.
Both Brunelleschi and Ghiberti were assigned deputies
on their employment as cathedral architects and master
builders in 1420. A drawing dating from 1426, by
Ghiberti's deputy Giovanni di Gherardo da Prato, has
been preserved. It is the only one of which we can be
sure that it dates from the time that the dome was built.
Da Prato clearly used it as material for his criticism of
Brunelleschi's work as architect and master builder. It is
highly unlikely that Ghiberti was unaware of the
intentions of his deputy. And although the cathedral
operai expressed their confidence in Brunelleschi, this
episode shows Brunelleschi's changed circumstances
from the time that he became involved with the
cathedral dome. Suddenly, after two decades, he was
exposed to jealousy and rivalry.

In addition he had to present a building program and
was obliged always to be present on the drum. The
program, which is still preserved today in the cathedral
museum, dates from 1420 and comprises twelve points.

It is the only document by Brunelleschi's own hand
which has been preserved. It contains a number of
remarkable ideas which are concerned with a wider
range of issues than simply the technical building work.
The dome was to consist of two vaults (ill. 95). The task
of the outer one was to protect the inner one from the
rain and to make the dome as such appear more grand.
With this double shell principle, Brunelleschi makes a
clear distinction between the body of space and the body
of the building. The latter is completed by the outer
calotte, the former by the inner one. That such a
construction principle takes the observer and visitor to
the church into account is obvious. If the church is
observed from the outside, the dome impresses with its
massive dimensions, if it is experienced from the inside,
the smaller dome preserves proportionality. It does not
overpower the visitor. Taking account of the various
modes of perception in this way is without precedent.
We can find no models for this either in classical
antiquity or in the Middle Ages. Twenty four ribs, *sproni*,
were to serve as horizontal and vertical struts for the two
domes. Brunelleschi envisaged one rib in each of the
corners, that is eight altogether, and two each on the
eight sides. Thus sixteen different ring anchors made
of stone, iron and wood serve the same purpose.
Brunelleschi wanted the shells of the dome and the

90 *Santa Maria del Fiore*, view from below of the mighty cathedral dome

The curvature of the dome was so designed by Brunelleschi that we do not lose sight of the lantern and the white ribs leading up to it even if we observe it from close by – looking upwards from the cathedral square.

91 *Santa Maria del Fiore,* detail of a marble rib, seen from the lantern

Eight of the 28 braces which Brunelleschi uses for the construction of the dome appear on the outside. Although these marble ribs do not perform any static functions, they give the effect of being part of a mighty clamp placed over the dome.

92 *Santa Maria del Fiore,* the interior of the dome

The space between the inner and outer shells of the dome, the former four meters thick and the latter 80 centimeters thin: the outer boundary of the inner shell can be seen to the right and the inner boundary of the outer shell to the left. The stairs leading to the lantern run in between.

93 *Santa Maria del Fiore*, interior of the dome

Example of the herringbone construction at the base of the lantern. The round window leads to the stairs running in the space between the two shells.

struts to be done in sandstone, *macigno*, and marl, *pietra forte*, but only to a certain height. From that point onwards bricks or tuffs were to be used because they are lighter. Marble ribs were to be set upon the outer shell (ill. 91), one in each corner, making eight once again. Brunelleschi saves the point that the dome is to be built without scaffolding to the last, and he concludes, convinced that there is nothing further to say, with the words: "Practice will show what further steps are necessary in the construction of the walls."

The simple and persuasive principle which Brunelleschi used was to lay the stones for the building not horizontally, but sloping inwards. Bodies leaning towards one another support each other. A new ring of the wall was only started when the last one had been completed, that is when all eight sections had reached the same height. The so-called herringbone work, *spina pesce*, (ills. 93, 94) in which the stones were linked did the rest. This kind of masonry work appears to have been known as early as the 14th century in Florence. The building history of Florence Cathedral is well documented. In some periods we have information on Brunelleschi's activities at almost fortnightly intervals. And yet questions remain. Some things which would be of interest to us today he might have kept to himself, other things were not documented because they were not thought to be important. Thus we know that the rising curve of the dome was specified but we do not know how Brunelleschi ensured that the exact calculation was implemented in practice. He had to be sure that none of the eight main ribs deviated from the specified circular form. What did he use to control the measurements? How did he transfer supplementary calculations, carried out on a piece of paper, to the mighty building? In answer to such and other similar questions, Vasari tells the story that Brunelleschi had transferred the section of the sphere – in its original size – to a sandbank in the Arno. Here a great variety of

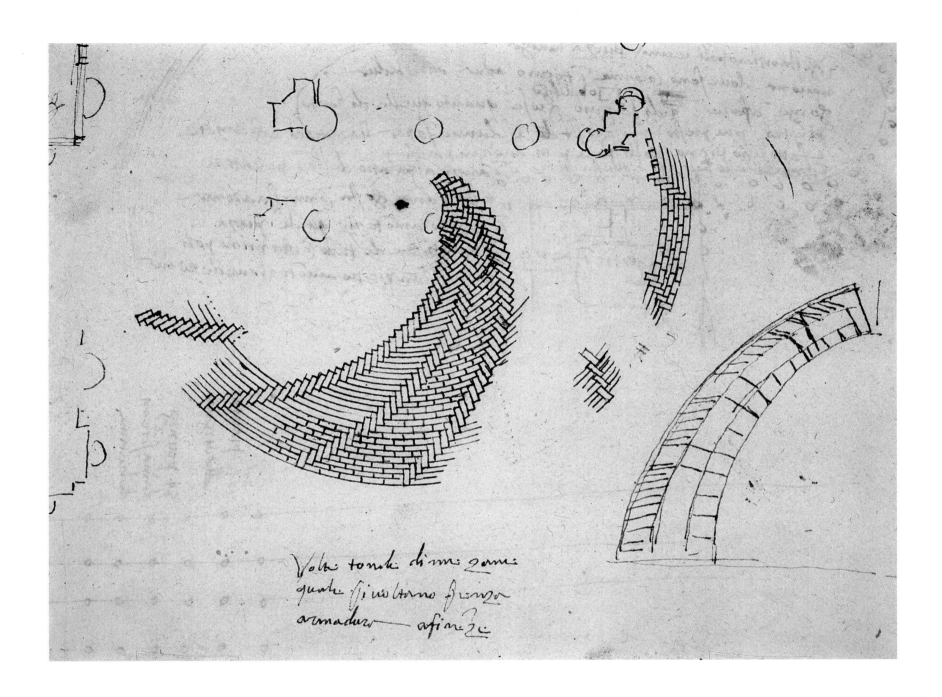

Volta tonda dimezane
quale si volterno firenza
armadure — afirenze

hypotheses appear in the literature. Did Brunelleschi work with the procedure which has become known as *calandrine con tre corte*? Or did he use *centine*, patterns, which were shaped in accordance with the *quinto-acuto* arch? How did he determine the central axis of the octagon if this was the case? Did he use so-called star chains, *stella*, as aids or perhaps an optical measuring instrument, a three armed protractor, the *gualandrino*? Was the central axis in the end simply found by putting an 80 meter high mast in position, as dome researchers were speculating as early as the 18th century?

The more we learn of Brunelleschi's work, the more our admiration grows for his knowledge of the possibilities offered by the various materials, his experience in construction techniques and in statics, and his ability to provide the mathematical foundation for the whole project.

The dome was consecrated on 30 August 1436. Florence Cathedral was worthily completed. Leon Battista Alberti could not contain his euphoria with regard to the dome: "Reaching steeply into the sky, it is so high that it embraces all the people of Tuscany in its shadow."

94 Antonio da Sangallo
Drawing for the construction of the dome using herringbone work
Pen-and-ink drawing, 28.5 x 43.2 cm
Galleria degli Uffizi, Gabinetto dei Disegni e delle Stampe, Florence

"With a domed vault made of bricks as is built in Florence without scaffolding," the inscription reads. On the one side, the sheet shows the double shell structure of the dome, on the other an example of the *spina pesce* technique, the herringbone construction.

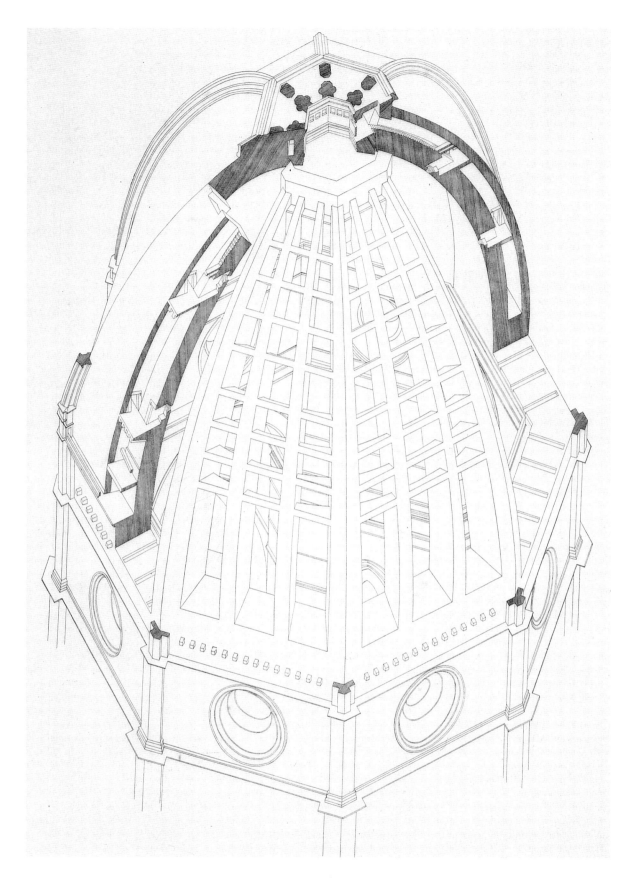

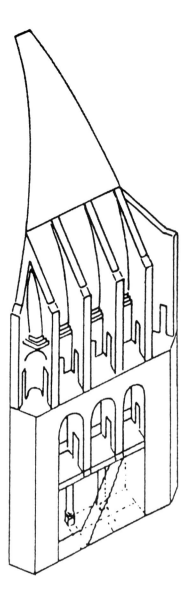

95 Axonometry of the dome structures of Santa Maria del Fiore and of San Giovanni, Cathedral and Baptistery of Florence (according to Sanpaolesi and Horn)

The double shell construction had its precursor in the Baptistery – but the axonometry only shows one side, not the complete structure of the dome. With the Baptistery, four braces on each side of the dome take the thrust of the vault. They are linked by standing barrel vaults which, together with the braces, reach about a third of the way up the dome. A framework of 32 braces thus supports the inner shell and surrounds the rising curvature. This design concept is used by Brunelleschi, but with key changes. The braces are replaced by colossal ribs which rise to the lantern. The brace design which acts from the outside is transformed by Brunelleschi into a self-supporting skeleton or ribs. Thus he creates quite different statics, as is clearly visible in the octagon corners. The braces of the Baptistery are attached directly to the vault from the edge of the bosses on two sides, and the groin runs down between them. Braces and dome remain independent elements although they are linked. Brunelleschi replaces this complicated corner solution with a single mighty rib which itself provides the transfer from the bosses and which carries the corner itself.

96, 97 (right and below) Wooden model of the lantern of *Santa Maria del Fiore*, 17th century
Museo dell'Opera del Duomo, Florence

The model is not Brunelleschi's original but one made in the 17th century which looks different. According to Manetti, Brunelleschi's *modello* merely indicated the construction and overall shape; the architect avoided reproducing any details or decorations for fear of envious persons and imitators.

98 (below) *Santa Maria del Fiore*, ground plan of lantern

If this ground plan is compared with the one for *Santa Maria degli Angeli* (ill. 81), it is immediately clear that both buildings are related. The supports on the inner polygon are found in both; their essential difference lies in the external polygon. The external wall from the earlier building is absent and further supports have taken the place of the niches. This has altered the character of the space decisively: a "chambered building" has become a "monument building" (Heydenreich).

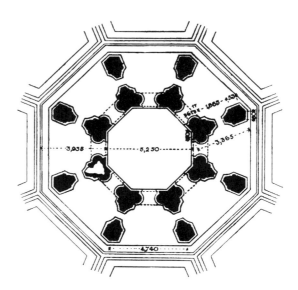

THE LANTERN

After the completion of the dome, a competition for the lantern was announced in 1436. It is surprising that such a competition should have been announced at all, for Brunelleschi, who had clearly been working on his proposal for the upper part of the dome in secret for some time, had already presented his model to the cathedral *operai*.

There is evidence that Brunelleschi started thinking about the lantern a long time beforehand. In order to provide the required base for his model, he had made the curvature of the dome somewhat steeper than was prescribed by the model of 1367. It must, however, be added that his *modello* was not necessarily the only reason for this divergence. A further reason may be that Brunelleschi wanted to make the red dome with its

white marble ribs visible in its full size (ill. 90). For it is due to this deviation from the model that the full upward extent of the ribs can be seen.

As Brunelleschi had brilliantly mastered the task of building the dome, he must have been deeply hurt by the fact that he did not immediately receive the commission to build the lantern. That this was not an unreasonable expectation can be illustrated by the example of Ghiberti. When the latter had completed the second Baptistery door in 1424, he was immediately commissioned to do the third one. No new competition was announced.

In the competition for the lantern, Brunelleschi was competing not only against Ghiberti, his former rival, but also against Manetti Ciaccheri, who built his wooden models. A comment by Brunelleschi on Ciaccheri's proposals is recorded which reveals a great

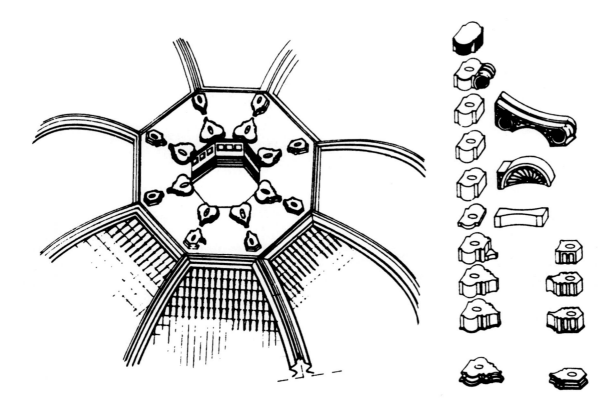

99 (left) *Santa Maria del Fiore*, the marble building stones for the base of the lantern and the buttresses (according to Borsi, Morolli and Quinterio)

The diagrammatic drawing shows the individual stones which were required. They were probably cut and processed in the quarries from Brunelleschi's drawings, at least according to Vasari. Only final corrections were thus carried out as the lantern was constructed.

deal about the former: "The next model that this man will build here will be mine."

In the end, Brunelleschi's proposal was accepted after all. A model, not the original one but a later copy of the lantern, can be seen in the cathedral museum today (ill. 96). The execution of the lantern continued, however, beyond 1471. The work was thus only concluded 25 years after Brunelleschi's death. His successors to the responsibility for the construction included Michelozzo (1446–1452) and Antonio Manetti (1452–1460). During his lifetime, Brunelleschi was able to complete little more than the plinth. Lengthy preparation of the building material – a pair of buttresses for example consists of 17 separately prepared marble pieces (ill. 99) – slowed the work down. But despite all of this the lantern is Brunelleschi's achievement alone.

Its lower storey alone makes it clear that we a dealing with a late work of his (ill. 100). Half columns are inserted between the main pillars and the buttresses are built in the form of a portal which is topped by a volute. The "weight of the forms" (Heydenreich) recalls *Santa Maria degli Angeli*. There are indeed references which connect the two buildings. We might say that Brunelleschi "repeats" the earlier ground plan but this time in transformation: "The *chambered* pillar construction of Angeli is inverted to become *non-chambered*" (Heydenreich). A chambered building has become a monument. A comparison of the ground plans makes this immediately clear (ills. 81, 98).

Brunelleschi's lantern is the cathedral's eye-catcher and has no architectural precedent. Its many medieval precursors always had the form of plain round aedicules. This applies not only to Brunelleschi's early works (cf. ills. 62, 71) but also to that major Florentine model, the Baptistery (ill. 88). The provision of buttresses, which form a transition from the ribs of the dome to the tip of the lantern, is a unique feature. Brunelleschi might have found the inspiration for this creation in pieces of gold work of the late Gothic and early Renaissance period, such as monstrances, holy vessels and the decoration on crosiers, with which he was familiar as a result of his training as an artist. But this would imply that Brunelleschi had transferred a small-scale form from applied art into large-scale architecture. The lantern also makes the volute into a constructive building element in Renaissance architecture. Due to Brunelleschi, it becomes an important part of the way that a façade is structured. We need only think of Alberti's structure for the façade of Santa Maria Novella in Florence, which was started in 1458. Brunelleschi's achievement lies in putting an old motif to use: the classical console. Like the latter, the volute mediates between the vertical and horizontal line.

100 (opposite) *Santa Maria del Fiore*, overall view of the lantern seen from Giotto's campanile, construction started 1436

The proportions of the lantern could hardly be more appropriate: "a little smaller and it would appear awkward and fail to offer sufficient counter-weight to the sweeping dome – a little bigger and it would grow to contradictory independence" (Klotz). With its slim arcades, in which the polygonal sides of the drum are concluded, and its sweeping buttresses, whose broad volutes take up the motion of the ribs, it lends the dome its appropriate height (ill. 87). The buttresses of the lantern represent the consistent continuation of the Gothic framework of ribs of the dome.

101 (left) *Santa Maria del Fiore*, detail view of the lantern

The pilasters are positioned at narrow intervals, the arches have a small reach. The massive volutes lick the pilasters, the principal cornice weighs heavily on them. The high round-arched attic with its interspersed cones is situated at the base of the roof covered in marble tiles.

102 (left) *Santa Maria del Fiore*, detail view of the lantern

The pilasters support the principal cornice, the inserted half-pillars carry the arches. Not until Brunelleschi's lantern does it become common in the Renaissance to combine the two building elements. The capitals of the half-pillars, the two leaf series with pearl and egg and dart, are unique in the architecture of the time. No less noticeable is the projecting entablature with its conspicuous elements such as for example the dentils. The design of the decoration undoubtedly represented a key problem for Brunelleschi. Ornaments of enormous dimensions had to be created in view of the height.

103 (opposite) *Santa Maria del Fiore*, detail view of the lantern (seen from the tip)

It is very easy to see from this perspective how well Brunelleschi has succeeded in creating a connection between the dome and the lantern through the buttress portal with its volute on top. The volutes, so to speak, repeat the upward motion of the marble ribs.

104 (opposite) *Santa Maria del Fiore* (lantern detail: a volute)

The volutes show how life-like vegetable forms can appear: the open leaf rosettes, the pods under whose surface the peas can be seen, and the fleshy leaves in the upper spandrel. Some specialists hold the view that one of Brunelleschi's successors is responsible for these decorations, namely Michelozzi Michelozzo.

105 (right) *Santa Maria del Fiore*, detail view of the lantern

The sweeping buttresses allow the view of an adjacent pillar. The way in which they were constructed from individual elements can be clearly seen.

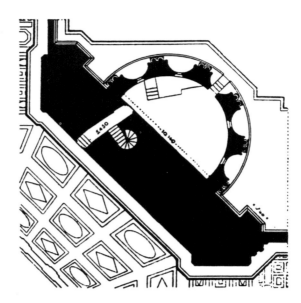

106 *Santa Maria del Fiore*, exedra, ground plan, from 1439

The exedra inscribe a complete semi-circle. Their façade is formed by six delicate double pillars which alternate with five niches let into the thick wall. This creates a very unusual ground plan.

THE EXEDRA

In 1438, Brunelleschi designed the four semi-circular exedra, the niches buried in a strong wall which flank the drum (ill. 108). Building began in the following year and the first was completed in 1444, though work continued until 1477. All four were not in place until long after Brunelleschi's death.

The exedra do not fulfil a constructional function, but serve purely as decoration. They emphasize another part of the building, the drum, through which the dome in turn rises above the church roof (ill. 89). It is in accord with the architectural intentions of the Renaissance "that the building should be raised on a plinth like a monument." (Klotz). With Brunelleschi's buildings this might be the flight of stairs leading up to the *Ospedale degli Innocenti*, or the building containing the hall of the Palazzo di Parte Guelfa; and, in this context, the pedestals of the *tribune morte* of the exedra.

This high plinth lifts them above the balustrade running around the whole building. The elongated capitals of the pillars give rise to the assumption that they were intended as a measure to compensate for their high position. They were made longer to prevent the danger of foreshortening. That this is the case is also shown by the imposts between the capitals and the entablature (ill. 109). Assuming that the observer stands below, they serve to create a clear separation between the two building elements. There is certainly no reason for them in this spot from a construction point of view. From the late classical period onwards, we always encounter imposts when arches and pillars are to be linked. Since it was necessary to keep to a strict separation of bearing and loading elements, a direct connection between pillar – a bearing element – and

arch – an element which is both bearing and loading – was inadmissible according to the architectural canon. The impost was thus inserted in "mediation". That Brunelleschi is aware of this rule is shown by the arcades of *San Lorenzo* (ill. 37).

Thus Brunelleschi, the discoverer of centralized perspective, takes account of the different ways of perception in his architectural designs. He takes into consideration the spatial position of people in relation to architecture. In response to the question whether the lantern could be seen from the Baptistery gate, Brunelleschi would probably have answered that a straight line simply had to be drawn between the two points. If the line does not meet any obstacles, such as a part of the building, the answer is yes. The exedra display a structure which points to the future. With them, half-pillars appear for the first time, and double ones here at that (ill. 110), on the outside of a Renaissance building. The route from these leads to the depictions of the ideal cities such as shown on the panel in Urbino (ill. 115) – ascribed to Piero della Francesca (ca. 1420–1492) – but also to the centralized buildings of the high Renaissance such as the Tempietto of San Pietro in Montorio built by Bramante in 1502.

Here, too, the niche, which was part of Brunelleschi's architecture from *San Lorenzo* (not executed) and *Santo Spirito* (executed) to *Santa Maria degli Angeli*, achieves its greatest formal clarity as a compositional element. That it appeared on the outside of the cathedral as part of the façade points Renaissance architecture to the future no less than the use of half-pillars.

The exedra convincingly round off the new appearance which Brunelleschi gave *Santa Maria del Fiore*, Florence Cathedral.

107 *Santa Maria del Fiore*, two exedra and one apse dome

The radial arrangement of the exedra with the hemispheric domes rising in between them to the same level completes the appearance of the cathedral that Brunelleschi had given it with the dome: the function performed by the lantern at the top is paralleled by the four exedra at its base.

108 *Santa Maria del Fiore*, an exedra

A high plinth lifts the exedra so far above the balustrade that even the bases of the pillars are visible. That is not the only construction measure which Brunelleschi uses to take account of the high position of his *tribune morte*. The capitals of the pillars are elongated and imposts were inserted between them and the entablature, whose task it is to contrast the two building elements with one another and to prevent the boundary between capital and entablature becoming blurred. In addition, the frame moldings of the niches and the decoration of the entablature are clearly brought out.

109 (opposite) *Santa Maria del Fiore*, exedra (detail: the Corinthian capitals of two pillars with impost and parts of the entablature)

110 (right) *Santa Maria del Fiore*, exedra (detail: a niche with two framing pairs of pillars)

The clarity which characterizes the exedra as one of Brunelleschi's late works is clearly visible in the details of the decoration: the proportions of the flutes of the attic bases, the geometrical stylization of the acanthus leaves at the capitals, the ornaments of the architrave and the striking ornament of the frieze.

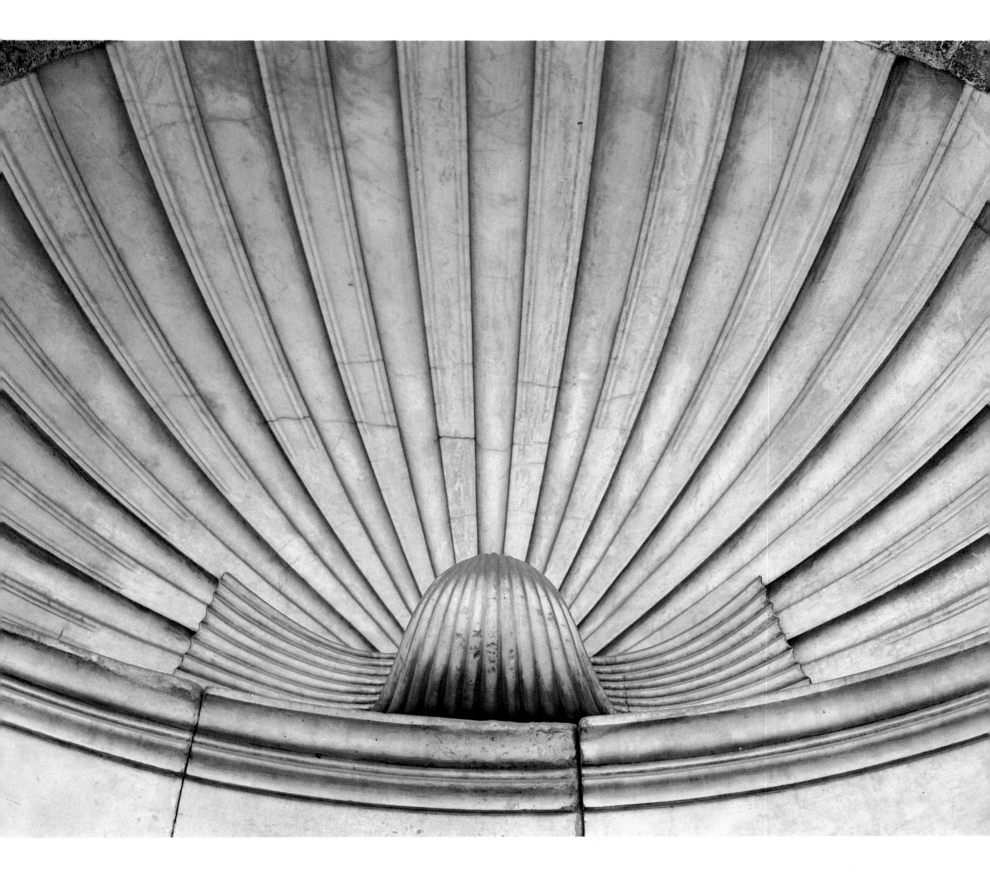

111 (opposite) *Santa Maria del Fiore*, detail view of an exedra

Brunelleschi accentuated the appearance of the exedra with black and white. The correspondingly decorated frieze emphasizes the semi-circle of the ground plan. However, the niches are also framed not just by moldings but also by the dark marble strips which trace their opening and depth in equal measure.

112 (above) *Santa Maria del Fiore*, exedra (detail: the shell calotte in a niche)

BRUNELLESCHI'S SIGNIFICANCE AS AN ARTIST

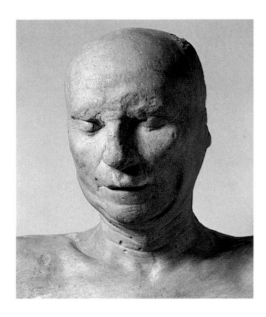

113 (above) *Filippo Brunelleschi's death-mask*, 1446
Plaster
Museo dell'Opera del Duomo, Florence

114 (opposite) Michelangelo and others
Dome, 1557 – 1593
San Pietro, Rome

The dome rests on a drum with 16 windows and has a diameter of 42.34 meters. It consists of an inner and an outer shell between which it is possible to climb up. On the inside alone the dome reaches a height of 119 meters. From 1546 onwards, Michelangelo tried, with several variations, to set out his ideas of this dome more precisely in models and drawings. His constantly revised plans reveal his inspiration: Brunelleschi's dome on Florence Cathedral. Michelangelo began work on a large wooden model in 1558, which shows the dome in its key elements as building had progressed since 1557. The drum was almost finished on the death of the artist in 1564, but construction of the dome was not begun until 1588. It was completed in 1590 and three years later it received its crowning lantern. Giacomo della Porta was the architect in charge.

Brunelleschi's buildings mark the beginning of the Renaissance in architecture. There is no doubt about that today, though his art was nevertheless not always judged in the same way. For the generation which succeeded him he was the renewer of classicism. Antonio di Pietro Averulino, better known as Filarete, wrote in 1464: "Blessed be the spirit of Filippo di Ser Brunellesco, who reintroduced this ancient way of building to our city, Florence, and brought it to life so that no other style is in common use today." Giorgio Vasari adds just under 100 years later: "And he deserves all the more praise as during his lifetime the German style was revered and practiced by all artists in the whole of Italy." This pointed remark is aimed at Gothic architecture, an indication of hostility which represents the negative side of the revival of the classical period.

Today Brunelleschi's position in the history of architecture is seen in a somewhat more subtle light, possibly because of our greater distance. Brunelleschi intensively studied the buildings in Florence and Tuscany for the whole of his life. It is not, therefore, surprising that many elements of his architecture tend to go back to the so-called proto-Renaissance of the 11th and 12th centuries rather than to the classical architecture which he also began to assimilate – albeit at a later time. However, the extent to which he restricts his selection from the rich choice on offer is remarkable in this context. It is the simple forms which he chooses: the plain Attic bases, the Corinthian capitals, the Corinthian pilasters with their sixfold fluting. When the cornicing above the architrave is decorated, it is with egg and dart or dentils – the richer ornaments on the exedra represent the proverbial exception. The architrave itself also shows an almost regular structure in the sequence of its fasciae width. That Brunelleschi also made use of Gothic structural principles is something which we are more inclined to acknowledge today than his biographer Manetti was.

What makes Brunelleschi stand apart, and what makes his application of the impressions he has gathered so impressive, is his "rational judgment as basis for his action" (Argan), his systematic rigor. It saves him from becoming a mere copyist – this applies both to the proto-Renaissance and classicism – and it saves him from losing sight of what architecture means for him. For Brunelleschi, its aesthetic and functional value is nourished by clarity of structure. To give one example (ill. 95): the double shelled dome has its precursor in the Baptistery in Florence. Here, Brunelleschi found the idea for such a construction. But he transformed the braces of the inner shell of the Baptistery into colossal ribs. By appearing merely to lengthen them, Brunelleschi created a rib structure which can no longer be compared with the "retaining supports" (Klotz) of the Baptistery; that includes any stylistic comparisons. For the dome of San Giovanni imitates the one on the Pantheon and lifts its support structure, which is hidden in the mass of the walls, up into a free-standing framework – albeit only in the lower third. It thus does no more than prepare for the rib structure of the cathedral dome. Brunelleschi then creates completely different statics by transforming the braces, thereby also changing the external appearance of the dome. It is no longer restrained, but can rise freely. The way in which Brunelleschi exploits this idea advances so far beyond the Baptistery's solution that we can create a further link from his dome to Michelangelo's for St. Peter's in Rome (ill. 114); the latter is undoubtedly the most important "successor" to Brunelleschi's dome.

Brunelleschi's concern in his architecture with people and their sensual reception – or perhaps can be seen above all – in the important role played by light as a constituent element of the way that space is formed; or, from the perspective of the observer, as an element in the experience of space. Another point applies in this connection: architecture is displayed in all its clarity, in its orderliness without rigidity, and in its complete harmony.

115 Piero della Francesca (?)
The Ideal City, ca. 1475
Tempera on wood, 60 x 200 cm
Galleria Nazionale delle Marche, Urbino

Piero della Francesca, who lived from 1420 to 1492 and visited
Florence for the first time in 1439, was already one of those artists
for whom the use of centralized perspective had become a matter of
course. He also concerned himself with the subject on a theoretical
level. His treatise "De prospectiva pingendi", which he wrote at the
end of his life, is the most detailed theory of perspective of the
Renaissance. The constructions in perspective on which *The Ideal
City* is based are probably based on the diagrams made for the
treatise. The painting is so closely connected with the ideas set out
by the painter that at the very least it must be assumed to be a work
originating in the circle around Piero della Francesca. It is evident
how much the round temple in the center of the city square owes to
Brunelleschi's late works, above all the exedra.

CHRONOLOGY

1377 Filippo Brunelleschi is born in Florence to Ser Brunellesco di Lippi and Giuliana Spini. His parents come from well-off families; his father is a respected notary. Brunelleschi's official name is probably Pippo di Ser Brunellesco Lippi.

Apart from his activities as a building specialist, advisor and planner of building projects, which also entailed travel to other cities, Brunelleschi would later execute his most important architectural work in his native city, Florence.

1378 Birth of Lorenzo Ghiberti.

1386 Donato di Niccolò di Betto Bardi, known as Donatello, is born in Florence.

1396 Michelozzi Michelozzo, properly Michelozzo di Bartolomeo, is born in Florence.

1397 Paolo di Dono, known as Uccello, is born in Florence.

1398 Brunelleschi seeks admission as a goldsmith to the Silk Merchants Guild (Arte della Seta), to which the goldsmiths belong.

1399 The Florentine goldsmiths Lunardo di Mazzeo and Piero Giovannino are commissioned to carry out the silver altar of St. Jacob for the Pistoia cathedral of San Zeno.

Brunelleschi works with them; the young artist creates the first of his works which have been preserved.

1399/1400 Luca della Robbia is born in Florence.

1401 The competition for the second door of the Baptistery of San Giovanni is announced in Florence. Ghiberti participates as well as Brunelleschi; the bronze reliefs of *The Sacrifice of Isaac* are created. Ghiberti wins the competition. Tommaso di Ser Giovanni Cassai, known as Masaccio, is born near Arezzo.

1404 Brunelleschi registers as a goldsmith with the Silk Merchants Guild, although he seems increasingly to concern himself with architecture.

Leon Battista Alberti is born in Genoa.

1404–1406 Brunelleschi is involved for the first time in work on Florence Cathedral, Santa Maria del Fiore, as the member of a commission of experts.

1409 Bernardo Rosselino is born near Florence.

1412 Birth of Andrea di Lazzaro Cavalcanti, the subsequently adopted son and pupil of Brunelleschi, known as Il Buggiano after his place of birth.

Brunelleschi is described as *capomaestro* in a document, which indicates that he had already worked for some time as an architect.

1415 Brunelleschi's studies on perspective fall into the middle of the second decade, including the *tavolette prospettiche*, the two panels of the Baptistery and the Piazza della Signoria with the Palazzo Vecchio, demonstrating perspective. We owe detailed descriptions of the two panels to Manetti and Vasari.

Donatello creates the relief and the statue of St. George for Or San Michele.

1417 Brunelleschi adopts Buggiano.

1418 The competition for the dome of Florence Cathedral, Santa Maria del Fiore, is announced. Lorenzo Ghiberti is once again among Brunelleschi's rivals, but loses this time.

1419 Work starts on the Ospedale degli Innocenti, the Foundling Hospital. Brunelleschi's presence at the building site is documented until 1427.

In the same year, Brunelleschi starts building the Barbadori Chapel in Santa Felicità.

The commission by Giovanni di Bicci de' Medici for the construction of the Old Sacristy, which is to serve the Medici as a mausoleum, is also dated to about 1419.

1420 Although he lost the competition, Lorenzo Ghiberti is appointed together with Brunelleschi as *operai*, cathedral architect and master builder, for the construction of the dome. Filippo presents his building program.

1421 Start of building work on San Lorenzo; it stops after only four years and is not resumed for another two decades.

1422 Antonio di Tuccio Manetti, Brunelleschi's biographer, is born.

1425 Ghiberti begins the execution of the *Paradise door* for the Baptistery in Florence. From 1425 to 1427 Masaccio creates his fresco of *The Holy Trinity*;

modern research generally accepts that Brunelleschi also worked on the fresco.

1428 Masaccio dies in Rome.

1429 Building work on the Old Sacristy of San Lorenzo is thought to have been completed in this year.
Brunelleschi starts planning the chapel for Andrea Pazzi in the monastery courtyard of Santa Croce. Work does not start until 1442, four years before Brunelleschi's death.
Giovanni di Bicci de' Medici dies. He leaves an enormous fortune to his son Cosimo.

1432 Brunelleschi journeys to Rome and stays in the Eternal City. Contrary to his biographer Manetti, who has Brunelleschi travel to Rome at the start of the century, our only evidence for such a journey is for this later time.

1434 Brunelleschi begins planning for his second big basilica, Santo Spirito. He will only live to see the start of the building work. Work on the centralized building Santa Maria degli Angeli starts; it stops again as early as 1437.
At the instigation of the Stonemasons Guild, the Arte della Pietra e Legname, in which he should have registered in his capacity as architect, but which he never did, Brunelleschi is arrested but soon released again.
Andrea della Robbia is born in Florence.

1435 Leon Battista Alberti publishes in Latin his treatise on painting, "De Pictura"; in the following year, he dedicates the Italian edition, "Della Pittura", to Brunelleschi.

1436 The dome of Florence Cathedral is completed. On 30 August it is consecrated during a ceremonial papal procession.
Brunelleschi presents his model for the lantern which does not, however, receive immediate approval. A competition, in which Brunelleschi once again encounters Ghiberti, is announced. Brunelleschi's proposal is finally accepted.

1439 Brunelleschi starts on the *tribune morte*, the exedra on the drum of the dome of the Cathedral. They will not be completed until long after his death.
Francesco di Giorgio is born in Siena.

1444 The humanist Carlo Massurppini becomes chancellor of the Florentine republic. Donato Bramante is born near Urbino.

1445 Giuliano di Sangallo is born in Florence.

1446 Filippo Brunelleschi dies on 15 April. His sole heir is Buggiano, even if the relationship between father and adopted son was never free of conflict.
At first, Brunelleschi was to be laid to rest in a tomb in a niche in Giotto's campanile, but then he is moved inside the cathedral.
Most of Brunelleschi's buildings were unfinished on his death: the lantern and the exedra of the cathedral, the basilicas of San Lorenzo and Santo Spirito, the Pazzi Chapel and Santa Maria degli Angeli, the Palazzo di Parte Guelfa.

1447 Erection of monument to Filippo Brunelleschi – inscription and tondo with picture – in Florence Cathedral, Santa Maria del Fiore.

GLOSSARY

abacus (Gk. *abax*, "slate"), in classical architecture, the slab on top of a column's capital.

aedicule (Lat. "small house"), an architectural frame for a shrine, niche, or window, consisting of two columns or pilasters supporting an entablature and pediment.

apse (Lat. *absis*, "arch, vault"), a semicircular projection, roofed with a half-dome, at the east end of a church behind the altar. Smaller subsidiary apses may be found around the choir or transepts. Also known as an **exedra**.

arcade (Lat. *arcus,* "arch"), a series of arches supported by columns, piers or pillars. In a **blind arcade** the arches are built into a wall.

arch, a curved, load-bearing structure in a wall opening that transfers the load to supports (pillars and columns). In classical, Romanesque and Renaissance architecture, arches are round; in Gothic architecture they are usually pointed. The inner surface of an arch is called the **intrados**; the triangular space between the outer curve of the arch and its architectural framework is called a **spandrel**. A **blind arch** is built into a wall.

architrave (It. "chief beam"), in classical architecture, the main beam resting on the capitals of a row of columns (ie the lowest part of the entablature); the molding around a window or door.

archivolt, a continuous decorative molding around an arch.

atrium open central courtyard, especially of a Roman house; a court in front of a church, usually one lined by a colonnade.

attic, in classical architecture, the storey above the main entablature. It was often decorated and was used to conceal the roofline. In classical architecture, the attic was often used on city gates and triumphal arches; in Renaissance architecture it was used on both churches and secular buildings.

Attic base, in classical architecture, the base of an Ionic column, consisting of two rings with convex edges linked by a concave molding.

aureole (Lat. [*corona*] *aureola*, "golden [crown]"), a circle of light shown surrounding a holy person, a halo.

baptistery (Gk. *baptisterion*, "wash basin"), from the 4th to the 15th centuries, a small building, usually separate from the main church, in which baptisms were performed. They were often circular or hexagonal, and dedicated to St John the Baptist. A well-known example is the Baptistery of the Duomo, the cathedral of Florence.

basilica (Gk. *basilike stoa*, "king's hall"), in Roman architecture a long colonnaded hall used as a court, a market or as a place for assemblies. The early Christians adopted this form of building for their churches, the first Christian basilicas being long halls with a nave flanked by colonnaded side aisles, and with an apse at the eastern end. With the addition of other features, in particular the transept, the basilica became the traditional Christian church.

bay, in architecture, a division of a building, either inside or out, which is created by supporting members such as walls, columns, buttresses etc.

bust, a sculpted portrait consisting of the head and shoulders. Developed in ancient Greece and widely used in ancient Rome, the bust was revived in 15th-century Italy.

buttress (Fr. *bouter*, "to thrust"), a vertical mass of masonry or brickwork built against a wall for support or reinforcement.

campanile (It. "bell tower"), a church bell tower, often standing detached from the body of the church. A well-known example is the campanile of St. Mark's Cathedral in Venice.

capital (Lat. *capitellum*, "little head"), the head or crowning feature of a column or pillar. Structurally, capitals broaden the area of a column so that it can more easily bear the weight of the arch or entablature it supports. They also provide an opportunity for decoration: medieval capitals, for example, were often richly decorated with sculptures of plants, animals, demons, faces or figures.

chapter house, a building in which the chapter (governing body) of a monastery of cathedral meet to conduct business.

choir (Gk. *khoros,* "area for dancing; chorus"), in a Christian church, the areas set aside for singers and the clergy, generally the area between the crossing and the high altar.

classical, relating to the culture of ancient Greece and Rome (**classical Antiquity**). The classical world played a profoundly important role in the Renaissance, with Italian scholars, writers, and artists seeing their own period as the rebirth (the "renaissance") of classical values after the Middle Ages. The classical world was considered the golden age for the arts, literature, philosophy, and politics. Concepts of the classical, however, changed greatly from one period to the next. Roman literature provided the starting point in the 14th century, scholars patiently finding, editing and translating a wide range of texts. In the 15th century Greek literature, philosophy and art – together with the close study of the remains of Roman buildings and sculptures – expanded the concept of the classical and ensured it remained a vital source of ideas and inspiration.

clerestory (or **clearstory**), in church architecture, the upper part of a nave, containing a row of windows.

cloister (Lat. *claustrum*, "an enclosed place"), a covered walk, with an open colonnade along one side, usually running along all four walls of the quadrangle of a monastery or cathedral.

conch (Lat. *concha*, "shell"), a small recess surmounted by a half-dome.

console, in classical architecture, an ornamental bracket carved (in profile) in an S-shape.

Corinthian, one of the three orders of classical architecture. See: **orders**

cornice, in architecture, a projecting moulding that runs around the top of a building, the wall of room, or other architectural feature.

crossing, in church architecture, the square space created by the intersection of the nave and the transepts. The crossing is usually covered by a tower or a dome.

crosier, a staff with a crook or cross at the end carried by a bishop or archbishop as a symbol of office.

dentil (Lat. *dent*, "tooth"), in classical architecture, a thin decorative molding beneath a cornice consisting of a row of small, regularly spaced rectangular blocks.

Dominicans (Lat. *Ordo Praedictatorum*, Order of Preachers), a Roman Catholic order of mendicant friars founded by St. Dominic in 1216 to spread the faith through preaching and teaching. The Dominicans were one of the most influential religious orders in the later Middle Ages, their intellectual authority being established by such figures as Albertus Magnus and St. Thomas Aquinas.

Doric, one of the three orders of classical architecture. See: **orders**

drum, in architecture, a cylindrical wall, sometimes pierced by windows, supporting a dome.

egg and dart, in classical architecture, a decorative motif consisting of carvings or paintings of alternate eggs and arrow-heads.

elevation, a scale drawing a building seen from the side (as opposed to from above, which gives the ground plan).

entablature, in classical architecture, the part of a building between the capitals of the columns and the roof. It consists of the architrave, the frieze, and the cornice.

exedra, in architecture, a recess, porch, or chapel projecting externally; an apse.

fasciae, sing. **fascia**, in classical architecture, the three horizontal bands – lying on top of one another, and projecting slightly from bottom to top – in an architrave.

fluting, closely spaced parallel grooves carved vertically in a column or pillar. In the Doric order the grooves meet in a sharp ridge; in the Ionic and Corinthian orders, they are separated by a narrow ridge.

Franciscans, a Roman Catholic order of mendicant friars founded by St. Francis of Assisi (given papal approval in 1223). Committed to charitable and missionary work, they stressed the veneration of the Holy Virgin, a fact that was highly significant in the development of images of the Madonna in Italian art. In time the absolute poverty of the early Franciscans gave way to a far more relaxed view of property and wealth, and the Franciscans became some of the most important patrons of art in the early Renaissance.

frieze (Lat. *frisium*, "fringe, embroidered cloth"), in classical architecture, the horizontal band of the entablature between the cornice and the architrave, often decorated with relief sculptures; a decorated band running along the upper part of an internal wall.

gallery, a platform or balcony projecting from the walls of a building; in church architecture, the upper story over a side aisle (in a basilica), over the ambulatory (centrally planned church), or over the west entrance.

Gothic (Ital. *gotico*, "barbaric, not classical"), the style of European art and architecture during the Middle Ages, following Romanesque and preceding the Renaissance. Originating in northern France about 1150, the Gothic style gradually spread to England, Spain, Germany and Italy. In Italy Gothic art came to an end as early as 1400, whilst elsewhere it continued until the 16th century. The cathedral is the crowning achievement of Gothic architecture, its hallmarks being the pointed arch (as opposed to the Romanesque round arch), the ribbed vault, large windows, and exterior flying buttresses. The development of Gothic sculpture was made possible by Gothic architecture, most sculptures being an integral part of church architecture. Its slender, stylized figures express a deeply spiritual approach to the world, though its details are often closely observed features of this world.

Great Schism (Gk. "separation, split"), a split in the Roman Catholic Church, 1378–1417, when there were two lines of papal succession, one in Rome and one (of the so-called antipopes) in Avignon in France.

homo quadratus (Lat. "human square"), in the system of architecture devised by the Roman architect Vitruvius, a basic unit of design based on the square a person was thought to make when standing upright with arms outstretched. This notion had a profound impact on Renaissance theories of architecture.

humanism, an intellectual movement that began in Italy in the14th century. Based on the rediscovery of the classical world, it replaced the Medieval view of humanity as fundamentally sinful and weak with a new and confident emphasis on humanity's innate moral dignity and intellectual and creative potential. A new attitude to the world rather than a set of specific ideas, humanism was reflected in literature and the arts, in scholarship and philosophy, and in the birth of modern science.

iconography (Gk. "description of images"), the systematic study and identification of the subject-matter and symbolism of art works, as opposed to their style; the set of symbolic forms on which a given work is based. Originally, the study and identification of classical portraits. Renaissance art drew heavily on two **iconographical** traditions: Christianity, and ancient Greek and Roman art, thought and literature.

impost, in architecture, the horizontal moulding or course of stone or brickwork at the top of a pillar or pier. Imposts often support arches.

intrados, the inner curve or underside of an arch.

lantern (Lat. *lanterna*, "lamp"), in architecture, a small turret that sits at the top of a dome or roof. Fitted with windows or openings, the lantern provides light to the space below.

Ionic, one of the three orders of classical architecture. See: **orders**

loggia (It.), a gallery or room open on one or more sides, its roof supported by columns. Loggias in Italian Renaissance buildings were generally on the upper levels. Renaissance loggias were also separate structure, often standing in markets and town squares, that could be used for public ceremonies.

lunette (Fr. "little moon"), in architecture, a semicircular space, such as that over a door or window or in a vaulted roof, that may contain a window, painting or sculptural decoration.

Mater Eleusa (Gk. "Mother of Compassion"), a depiction of the Madonna and Christ Child in which Christ holds his cheek against Mary's.

medallion, in architecture, a large ornamental plaque or disc set into a wall.

Minerva Medica, a Roman building of the 3rd century AD that was long thought to be a temple, though it is more likely to have been a pavilion in the garden of a villa. A domed building with apses on all sides, it was used as a model for early centralized churches.

modello (It. "model"), a drawing of a proposed painting, sculpture or building, often executed for the patron's approval. They were often highly finished and the design could be transferred to the canvas or wall by means of a grid drawn over the *modello* (**squared *modello***) and then scaled up.

monstrance (Lat. *monstrare*, "to show"), in the Roman Catholic Church, the receptacle in which the Host is held in order to be shown to the congregation.

oculus pl. **oculi** (Lat. "eye"), in architecture, a circular opening in a wall or at the top of a dome.

orders of architecture, in classical architecture, the three basic styles of design. They are seen in the form of the columns, capital, and entablatures. The earliest, the **Doric** order, was the simplest, with a sturdy, fluted column and a plain capital. The **Ionic** order had a slenderer column, a more elaborate base, and a capital formed by a pair of spiral scrolls. The **Corinthian** order was the most ornate, having a tall, very slender column and a capital formed of ornately carved leaves (acanthus).

Pantheon, temple built in Rome about 25 BC by Emperor Agrippa. Having a circular plan, and spanned by a single dome, it was one of the most distinctive and original buildings of ancient Rome.

pediment, in classical architecture, the triangular end of a low-pitched roof, sometimes filled with relief sculptures; especially in Renaissance and Baroque architecture, a decorative architectural element over a door or window, usually triangular (broad and low), but sometimes segmental.

pendentive, a curving and concave triangular section of vaulting linking a dome to the square base on which it rests.

perspective (Lat. *perspicere*, "to see through, see clearly"), the method of representing three-dimensional objects on a flat surface. Perspective gives a picture a sense of depth. The most important form of perspective in the Renaissance was **linear perspective** (first formulated by the architect Brunelleschi in the early 15th century), in which the real or suggested lines of objects converge on a vanishing point on the horizon, often in the middle of the composition (**centralized perspective**). The first artist to make a systematic use of linear perspective was Masaccio, and its principles were set out by the architect Alberti in a book published in 1436. The use of linear perspective had a profound effect on the development of Western art and remained unchallenged until the 20th century.

pilaster (Lat. *pilastrum*, "pillar"), a rectangular column set into a wall, usually as a decorative feature.

plinth (Gk. *plinthos*, "stone block"), in architecture, the block or slab on which a column, pedestal, or statue rests.

porch, a covered entrance to a building.

portal (Lat. *porta*, "gate"), a doorway, entrance, usually decorated.

portico (Lat. *porticus*, "porch"), a roofed space in front of an entrance, the roof often supported by columns.

proportions (in Renaissance architecture), the ratios of individual building elements to one another and to the building as a whole. Several systems were used. The *canon*, derived from classical architecture: the basic ratio was that of the human head to the body (1:7 or 1:10). The *golden mean,* derived from classical thought, based on the division of a line A into a smaller section C and a larger one B such that C it to B as B is to A. *Quadrature*, in which the square is the basic unit of design; and *triangulation*, in which the equilateral triangle is used to fix important points of design. *Harmonic* proportion employed music as a basis of design, with musical intervals expressed in terms of the ratios of string length and frequency establishing architectural ratios: eg octave = 1:2, fifth = 2:3, fourth = 3:4 etc,

quatrefoil (Fr. "four leaves"), a four-lobed architectural ornament or decorative motif, especially in Gothic window tracery.

relief (Lat. *relevare*, "to raise"), a sculptural work in which all or part projects from the flat surface. There are three basic forms: low relief (*bas-relief, basso rilievo*), in which figures project less than half their depth from the background; medium relief (*mezzo rilievo*), in which figures are seen half round; and high relief (*alto rilievo*), in which figures are almost detached from their background.

respond, in architecture, a half pillar (or corbel), set into a wall, that supports one side of an arch.

Romanesque (Lat. *romanus*, "Roman"), a style in Western art from the end of the 8th century to the 12th century, ie in the period immediately before Gothic era. Predominantly an architectural style, it is characterized by heavy, monumental construction and the use of the round arch. In painting and sculpture (almost entirely religious) figures are highly stylized, linear, and elongated.

rosette, a small architectural ornament consisting of a disc on which there is carved or molded a circular, stylized design representing an open rose.

sacristy (Lat. *sacer,* "sacred"), a storeroom attached to a church, generally used for housing vestments and sacred vessels.

sarcophagus, pl. **sarcophagi** (Gk. "flesh eating"), a coffin or tomb, made of stone, wood or terracotta, and sometimes (especially among the Greeks and Romans) carved with inscriptions and reliefs.

singers gallery (in Italian **cantoria**, pl. **cantorie**), a small gallery for singers or musicians, usually in a church. Two outstanding examples are those by the sculptors Andrea della Robbia and Donatello in Florence cathedral, both of which have richly carved marble panels.

spandrel, (1) a triangular wall area between two arches and the cornice or moulding above them, or between the curve of an arch and the rectangular frameworks around it (for example at the top of an arched doorway; (2) a curved triangular area between the ribs in a vault.

spina pesce (It. "fish spine"), a herringbone pattern in brickwork or tiles created by rows of short, slanting parallel lines, with the direction of the slant alternating row by row.

stucco (It.), a protective coat of coarse plaster applied to external walls; plaster decorations, usually interior. During the Renaissance stucco decorative work. often employing classical motifs, achieved a high degree of artistry.

tabernacle (Lat. "tent, hut"), in a church, a container for the consecrated host or relics, usually placed in the middle of an altar. Also, a small niche for statues.

tempera (Lat. *temperare*, "to mix in due proportion"), a method of painting in which the pigments are mixed with an emulsion of water and egg yolks or whole eggs (sometimes glue or milk). Tempera was widely used in Italian art in the 14th and 15th centuries, both for panel painting and fresco, then being replaced by oil paint. Tempera colors are bright and translucent, though because the paint dried very quickly there is little time to blend them, graduated tones being created by adding lighter or darker dots or lines of color to an area of dried paint.

terracotta (It. "baked earth"), fired clay that is unglazed. It is used for architectural features and ornaments, vessels, and sculptures.

tondo, pl. **tondi** (It "round"), a circular painting or relief sculpture. The tondo derives from classical medallions and was used in the Renaissance as a compositional device for creating an ideal visual harmony. It was particularly popular in Florence and was often used for depictions of the Madonna and Child.

topos, pl. **topoi** (Gk. "a commonplace"), in literature, figure of speech; in art, a widely used form, model, theme or motif; a familiar example.

transept, in church architecture, the two lateral arms that project from the nave to form the shape of a cross.

tribune, in church architecture, an apse. The *tribune morte* are the four semi-circular apses the architect Brunelleschi built in the angle of the nave and transepts of Florence cathedral to help to bear the weight of the cathedral's huge dome.

triumphal arch, in the architecture of ancient Rome, a large and usually free-standing ceremonial arch way built to celebrate a military victory. Often decorated with architectural features and relief sculptures, they usually consisted of a large archway flanked by two smaller ones. The triumphal archway was revived during the Renaissance, though usually as a feature of a building rather than as an independent structure. In Renaissance painting they appear as allusion to classical antiquity.

tympanum (Lat. "drum"), in classical architecture, the triangular area enclosed by a pediment, often decorated with sculptures. In medieval architecture, the semi-circular area over a door's lintel, enclosed by an arch, often decorated with sculptures or mosaics.

uomo universalis (It.), the Renaissance "universal man", a many-talented man with a broad-ranging knowledge of both the arts and the sciences.

varietas (Lat. "variety"), in Renaissance art theory, a work's richness of subject matter.

vault, a roof or ceiling whose structure is based on the arch. There are a wide range of forms, including: the barrel (or tunnel) vault, formed by a continuous semi-circular arch; the groin vault, formed when two barrel vaults intersect; and the rib vault, consisting of a framework of diagonal ribs supporting interlocking arches. The development of the various forms was of great structural and aesthetic importance in the development of church architecture during the Middle Ages.

volute (Lat. voluta), a scroll-shaped architectural ornament. It was first used on Ionic capitals, and reappeared during the Renaissance, when it was sometimes used to decorate a support for a pediment or the drum of a dome.

SELECTED BIBLIOGRAPHY

Argan, Giulio: Brunelleschi, Milan 1955

Behles, Joseph: Das Gestaltungsprinzip Brunelleschis beim Bau von Santo Spirito in Florenz, Frankfurt 1978

Borsi, Franco; Gabriele Morolli and Francesco Quinterio: Brunelleschiani, Rome 1979

Braunfels, Wolfgang:Drei Bemerkungen zur Geschichte und Konstruktion der Florentiner Domkuppel, in: Mitteilungen des Kunsthistorischen Instituts in Florenz 11 (1963–1965), pp. 203–226

Braunfels, Wolfgang: Brunelleschi und die Kirchenbaukunst des frühen Humanismus, Basel and Frankfurt 1981, (= 17th lecture of the Aeneas Silvius Foundation)

Brunelleschi, Filippo: La sua opera e il suo tempo. 2 Vols., Florence 1980 (= Atti del Convegno Internazionale di Studi, Firenze, 16–22 ottobre 1977)

Gombrich, Ernst: Antike Regeln und objektive Kriterien. Von der Schrift- und Sprachreform zur Kunst der Renaissance: Niccolò Niccoli und Filippo Brunelleschi, in: Gombrich, Ernst: Die Entdeckung des Sichtbaren, Stuttgart 1987, pp. 114–135

Gombrich, Ernst: The Story of Art, London 1995

Heydenreich, Ludwig Heinrich: Spätwerke Brunelleschis, in: Jahrbuch der Preußischen Kunstsammlungen 52 (1931), pp. 1–8

Klotz, Heinrich: Filippo Brunelleschi. The early works and the medieval tradition, London 1990

Manetti, Antonio and Filippo di Tuccio: Brunelleschi, edited by Heinrich Holtzinger, Stuttgart 1887

Manetti, Antonio: The life of Brunelleschi, Tr. by Catherine Enggass with an introduction, notes and critical text edition by Howard Saalman, London 1970

Paatz, Elisabeth and Walter: Die Kirchen von Florenz, 4 Vols., Frankfurt 1940 ff.

Paatz, Elisabeth and Walter: Die Kunst der Renaissance in Italien, Stuttgart 1953

Panofsky, Erwin: Die Perspektive als "symbolische Form", in: Panofsky, Erwin: Aufsätze zu Grundfragen der Kunstwissenschaft, edited by Hariolf Oberer and Egon Verheyen, Berlin 1985, pp. 99–167

Pizzigoni, Attilio: Filippo Brunelleschi, Zurich and Munich 1991

Saalman, Howard: Filippo Brunelleschi. The Buildings, London 1993

Sanpaolesi, Piero: Brunelleschi, Milan 1962

Schedler, Uta: Giovanni di Bicci, Filippo Brunelleschi und der Bau von San Lorenzo in Florenz, in: Münchner Jahrbuch der bildenden Kunst, 3rd Issue XLIV (1993), pp. 47–71

Vasari, Giorgio: Leben der ausgezeichnetsten Maler, Bildhauer und Baumeister
Tr. by Ludwig Schorn and Ernst Förster, edited with an introduction by Julian Kliemann, Worms 1988

Vasari, Giorgio: Lives of the Artists, Tr. by George Bull, Harmondsworth 1965

Wittkower, Rudolf: Grundlagen der Architektur im Zeitalter des Humanismus, Munich 1969

PHOTOGRAPHIC CREDITS

DATE DUE

MAR 1 2002		
MAR 4 2002		
MAY 1 0 2004		

GAYLORD   #3523PI   Printed in USA